### IS NOT A POSTURE MANUAL...

"In learning the Alexander Technique, you must at the outset dismiss from your mind all shining examples of good posture. The effort to hang on to some deliberate position, no matter what kind, is continuous and involves both physical and mental fatigue.

"It is in fact quite absurd to think of attaining some ideal posture and then clinging to it through all your subsequent activity. You are not a statue to be propped about in various juxtapositions to meet the changing requirements of whatever you are engaged in."

### ...OR AN EXERCISE PROGRAM...

"The word 'movement' as used here has nothing to do with the 1-2-3-4! 1-2-3-4! fitness exercises you did in gym class. It is in no way related to muscle-snapping, joint-wrenching gyrations of any kind. It provides, rather, a guideline to follow: a new way of thinking and moving."

### ...OR DIFFICULT

"Some people are reluctant to believe that anything remarkable can result from the Alexander Technique unless they do something that demonstrates huge effort. It is perhaps part of our American credo to believe that only prodigious feats can produce worthwhile results. Here, though, is one case where the big results come from a tiny change. The new science of chaos describes the butterfly effect, where it is possible that a movement as tiny as a butterfly flapping its wings in Brazil may ultimately cause a dramatic change in the outcome of weather in Nebraska. And so it is with the Alexander Technique: your ruler may not detect the difference, but you will feel it in every bone in your body."

# *The*
# ALEXANDER
## *Technique*

*Learning to Use Your Body
for Total Energy*

## SARAH BARKER

**BANTAM BOOKS**
*New York • Toronto • London • Sydney • Auckland*

# For Marj

THE ALEXANDER TECHNIQUE:
Learning to Use Your Body for Total Energy

A BANTAM BOOK / AUGUST 1978
REVISED EDITION / JANUARY 1991

*Photographs courtesy of Susan and Reed Erskine/
and Howard Wechsler.*

ISBN 0-553--28827-X

Published simultaneously in the United States and Canada

Bantam Books are published by Bantam Books, a division of Bantam Doubleday
Dell Publishing Group, Inc. Its trademark, consisting of the words "Bantam Books"
and the portrayal of a rooster, is Registered in U.S. Patent and Trademark Office
and in other countries. Marca Registrada. Bantam Books, 666 Fifth Avenue, New
York, New York 10103.

PRINTED IN THE UNITED STATES OF AMERICA

OPM     0 9 8 7 6 5 4 3 2 1

# Contents

# Acknowledgments

Before undertaking to write a "how to" book on the Alexander Technique, I thought long and hard: The idea of learning the Technique from a book seemed revolutionary and possibly heretical. Then I remembered that its originator, F. M. Alexander, had on his own discovered how to control the use of his body. Surely, the rest of us, even lacking his genius, could learn how, if given a set of sure guidelines.

When I began the necessary exploring and investigation for the original edition of this book, I received the help of innumerable people to whom I am most grateful. I would like to thank the various Alexander teachers with whom I have studied and spent long hours in discussion; and all my students, especially those who patiently suffered and, hopefully, benefited from the teaching experiments I conducted in the preparation of this book. Special acknowledgment is due my colleagues and associates at Rancho Linda Vista in Arizona, who supported me with their probing questions;

and thanks are also due to a number of close friends, who were always available for the encouragement and energy needed to carry on.

In the more than a decade since the first edition of this book, innumerable colleagues, associates, and mentors have enriched my understanding of how to communicate the principles of successful human achievement. While I can not name them all, I send them my thanks. My deepest appreciation goes to Webster University, Shakespeare and Company in Lenox, Massachusetts, Washington University and the University of Pittsburgh where I am currently a faculty member. All these places provided me with a helpful environment in which to expand my abilities. I am also grateful to the thousands of students whom I have taught and who have taught me. I am very thankful for my husband, Jerred Metz and my daughter, Ravenna who are a source of strength and joy. Special acknowledgment is due my master teacher, Marjorie Barstow who never ceases to be my inspiration.

My colleague, Peter Trimmer of Washington, D.C., graciously and expertly collaborated with me in demonstrating for the photographs that illustrate this book. For this revised edition Meredith Stead and John Knapp, New York teachers, have likewise offered their help in demonstrating for additonal photographs.

I am also indebted to several distinguished scholars in the field, upon whose work I have drawn freely, and whose individual help in some cases was indispensable to me.

I am grateful to Professor Nikolaas Tinbergen, of Oxford University, for his remarkable speech accepting the 1973 Nobel Prize in Medicine, which places the Alexander Technique in a modern scientific perspective; to Professor Raymond A. Dart, Professor Emeritus of Anatomy and Dean Emeritus of the Medical Faculty of the University of Witwatersrand, South Africa, for the insights in his *Anatomist's Tribute to F. Matthias Alexander;* to Dr. Frank Pierce Jones, Research Associate at the Tufts Institute for Psychological Research, whose studies of the Alexander Technique have accomplished much for the scientific understanding of this work; to Dr. Wilfred Barlow for his informative accounts of the medical use of the Technique in treating patients; to Edward Maisel, whose study introducing *The Alexander Technique: The Essential Writings of F. Matthias Alexander* (new revised edition, Lyle Stuart, Inc. 1989), an indispensable selection of Alexander's writings, has contributed so greatly to public appreciation of the Alexander Technique. In a couple of spots, I have, with Maisel's generous permission, closely paraphrased a few passages from that study. In the preface to his latest edition Maisel cites and quotes from Alexander's own words of encouragement to self-learners of the Technique, which provided new incentive for me to expand this work.

The greatest debt of all must be to Alexander himself, who laid down the guidelines for those of us who have followed him.

This book is not intended to reflect the views of any of the considerable number of people who helped me. The project is entirely my own.

SARAH BARKER

# PART I

# *Learning About the Alexander Technique*

## THE IMPORTANT BENEFITS IT OFFERS YOU

# I

# *The Alexander Technique: The What and the Why*

Imagine a technique for transforming the operation of your body, so simple that you can learn it yourself, a technique so amazing in its results that your physical and emotional life will soon change for the better, like the opening of a door into another world. That technique is the Alexander Technique, named for its discoverer, F. Matthias Alexander, and known around the world as one of the most extraordinary discoveries of our time.

## Scientific Acclaim

It would surprise many people to realize what the Alexander Technique can do for them were its astonishing results not supported by the most respectable scientific authority. During the years before and after Alexander's death in 1955, his students and followers conducted a considerable amount of research to substantiate his findings. At the Tufts Institute for Experimental Psychology, twenty-five years of investigations—using quantitative measure and control groups—have thrown important light on the manner in which the Alexander Technique produces its seemingly miraculous effects. There has also accumulated an impressive volume of clinical data, reports by physicians attesting to its remarkable effectiveness in helping many of their patients.

## Feeling at Your Best

Apart from suffering any specific medical symptoms, most of us plod through our days and nights in a condition far below optimum. We "manage"; we "get by." Good health is regarded as merely the absence of sickness. Against this keep-your-nose-above-water-level definition of being alive, the Alexander Technique proposes, as normal, an exuberant and vital sense of wellness: physical freedom and ease combined with mental flexibility and alertness.

Ours is an era where people have begun to value their bodies as unique and wonderful. We have learned that there is no mechanical device in the world—electronic, computerized or laser-beamed—that functions with such infinite resilience or so many delicate capacities as the human body. Many of us know now that through ignorance and insensibility we unnecessarily limit ourselves in how we function, and that today, more than ever, humanity's chance to survive may depend upon how men and women salvage themselves.

Indeed, this factor may prove more critical than our ability to manipulate the environment further. Just as we have thoughtlessly depleted the natural resources of the planet, so too are we daily abusing the most valuable resource of all—our bodies—and depleting our own energies. We scarcely begin to realize our enormous potential.

## Age Is No Barrier

If you think you're too old to begin learning anything so revolutionary, you're wrong. It's never too late. Even after forty or fifty years of continually misusing yourself, you can begin to make a beneficial and healthy change. John Dewey, one of the founding fathers of scientific philosophy and modern education, took up the Alexander Technique at the age of fifty-eight. He thereupon underwent an extraordinary rejuvenation and lived another thirty-five rich, full years. The ninety-two-year-old Dewey attributed this vital longevity to his Alexander practice. George Bernard Shaw learned the Technique at eighty and lived to ninety-four.

## If You Are Overweight

You can even streamline your physical appearance by means of the Alexander Technique. Something crucial is missing from our national quest for a more attractive physique. We have sufficient data on calories, diets and the dangers of eating too much. And we have information about fitness, aerobics and strenuous exertion. But little or nothing is ever mentioned about another important factor, which determines success in attaining a beautifully proportionate body. What about the way we wear our weight, whatever it may be? Why is it that two people of identical poundage and the same general build often have quite different looking torsos, one possessing a true waist and chest, the other a nondescript but thickening bulge? A beneficial side effect of the Alexander Technique is a better carriage of the body's weight. You appear more streamlined and proportioned.

## Your Rampant Emotions

All of us are subject to "states" of various kinds, and it is hardly news that human development in general is retarded by fear reflexes unduly excited by emotions, prejudices and fixed habits. What many authorities therefore find most impressive about the Alexander Technique is embodied in Aldous Huxley's statement that "If you teach an individual to be aware of his physical organism and then to use it as it was meant to be used, you can often change his entire attitude to life and cure his neurotic tendencies."

Huxley might have given his own story as a case in point. The famous writer had spent all his days in a state of acute physical illness until he studied the Alexander Technique and transformed himself. He had begun to withdraw from people, finding his physical and mental energies too drained by social contact, and he was beset by a terrible depression and a chronic insomnia that made it almost impossible to work. He had tried gardening, yoga and other remedies in vain, but it was the Alexander Technique that opened up a new way to live.

Can the Technique really help with our mental and emotional problems? Professor Frank Pierce Jones, the foremost scientific investigator among Alexander scholars, observed that while the physical effects of the Technique are indeed remarkable, "the psychological effects are of greater importance." Some of these, he noted, may of course be explained as the happy side effects of any betterment in physical condition, for a change in mental attitude often accompanies an increase in health. Individuals who suffer from chronic depression have found that when they change their bodies from a depressed posture to an open and balanced state their feelings of depression fade. There is likewise an improvement in our self-image when we feel more competent physically. We also discover how much more we like other people when we have a more relaxed feeling about ourselves.

But quite apart from these desirable side effects, reported in other therapies as well, Jones observed in his own experience "an almost immediate increase in mental and emotional control." This is because the Alexander Technique gives a workable approach in attacking emotional problems directly, and we are no longer simply at the mercy of confusion, worry, anger, panic.

## Living Without Stress

We can see how this works easily enough. Next time you're angry, notice whether you clench your hands slightly or perhaps a great deal. When angry, you may also hunch your shoulders and hold your chest rigidly. Or if you're anxious about something, you may find yourself making fidgety movements.

These are all surface reactions we can observe. Underneath are the unconscious tension states that can build into attitudes which interfere in our relationships with other people.

When you release those clenched fists, or prevent the

fidgeting, by means of the Alexander Technique, you may find your feelings much more within your control, because you are no longer reinforcing them with body tension.

Once you break this cycle of reinforcing feeling with body tension, you may even find that you no longer experience any disquiet—except perhaps to wonder where your rage or panic went. Thus freed, you are able to experience emotions fully in a few moments and begin thinking clearly again.

This new conscious control of yourself does not prevent you from feeling any emotional states—life would be rather stiff and boring if it did—but you will be able to allow for more appropriate and spontaneous responses to the events of your life if you are not locked into one fearful or angry response for all occasions.

## Being Who You Are

The Alexander Technique has particular value for people who don't want to fill themselves with drugs, or to shop from therapy to therapy, hoping for some kind of emotional relief. Millions of people exist in this half-alive state, countering their depressions and anxieties with a whole arsenal of tranquilizers, and moving hopefully from one fad to another. If they turn to the Technique, there is no magic formula that will instantly solve their problems. Instead, they will discover they have some choice in their lives and that they can consciously interrupt the debilitating habits of a lifetime. Freedom and ease is at their command.

## Beneficial Effects in Many Diseases

Many people would find it hard to believe the seemingly fantastic medical cures attributed to the Alexander Technique except that these extraordinary reports come from reputable physicians and scientists.

In 1973, Professor Nikolaas Tinbergen, upon receiving the Nobel Prize for Medicine, devoted half his acceptance speech to the Technique. He related how his interest in it was excited by a little experiment he had tried with his own family. He, his wife and one of their daughters had learned the Technique at the same time. As their body musculature began to function differently, they observed "with growing amazement" the marvelous results. They noted, for example, that the Technique brought about "very striking improvements in such diverse things as high blood pressure, breathing, depth of sleep, overall cheerfulness and mental alertness, resilience against outside pressure, and also in such a refined skill as playing a stringed instrument."

Tinbergen went on to affirm the possibility that certain other stress-related ailments could benefit from the Technique: rheumatism, including various forms of arthritis; respiratory ailments, even asthma; circulation defects that may lead to high blood pressure and heart conditions; gastrointestinal disorders of many types; sexual failures; migraines and depressive states that often lead to suicide. All these as well as other non-bug diseases, he suggested, might be helped by the Alexander Technique.

Tinbergen concluded that while the Technique is assuredly no cure-all to be applied in every case, "there can be no doubt that it often does have profound and beneficial effects; and I repeat once more, both in the mental and somatic sphere."

A physician, Dr. Wilfred Barlow, conducted a survey of men and women who had long used the Alexander Technique, and reported that in this group there were no coronaries, no cancers, no strokes, no rheumatoid arthritis, no slipped discs, no ulcers, no neurological disorders and no severe mental disorder. Barlow called this statistic "almost unbelievable" and concluded that 99 percent of the population need the Technique.

The *British Medical Journal* once published a letter, signed by nineteen doctors, endorsing the Technique for its remarkable effectiveness in the treatment of many of their patients, and called upon their profession to recognize and evaluate it. Unfortunately, no such evaluation has thus far been carried out, which is a point that must be emphasized. Although there has accumulated an impressive volume of personal testimony, no thoroughgoing scientific investigation has been conducted into any of the medical claims that have been made for the Technique.

A word of caution is therefore in order. If you have any ailment or illness—even one due to, or complicated by, the continual wear you place upon yourself through bad muscular habits—only your own physician can advise you if the Alexander Technique is likely to help.

## Everyone Can Use It

People from all walks of life benefit from the Alexander Technique. Those who have a professional interest in their bodies—actors, dancers, athletes—are making it an important part of their training and maintenance program. Leading performing arts conservatories and university programs schedule regular classes in the Alexander Technique for students. Many professional musicians attribute quick recovery and continuing ease in playing to their study of the Technique. Patients in medical institutes in London, New York and elsewhere find it acceptable as a valuable resource in physiotherapy. High fashion magazines, like Vogue and Harper's Bazaar, have informed their readers of what the Technique will do for presentation and appearance.

Trial projects in elementary and secondary schools throughout the western world have shown that the Alexander Technique significantly contributes to greater cooperation, attention, and self-esteem. John Dewey, the great educational philosopher and innovator, emphasized that only by including the Alexander Technique in the education of young children can we make that education truly effective.

## A Simple Method

This book will introduce you to the Alexander process of thinking and moving. It presents a simple method for learning the Technique by yourself. In the words of Professor Frank Jones, "Since the Alexander Technique is nothing more than the application of experimental method to problems of everyday behavior, there is no reason to delay the undertaking if a teacher is not available."

In Part I, the Alexander principle has been encapsulated in one very simple action called the Basic Movement (Chapter IV). It provides a compass for navigating in whatever physical or mental perplexities you may find yourself. It offers a key for orienting yourself in all that you do. Whether seated in a theater or standing waiting for a bus, you may readily apply it.

Part II presents a systematic program of seven easy Actions that shows you how to expand the Basic Movement as the basis for improving the quality of all the activities of your everyday life. These Actions will facilitate this because they are invariably involved in almost everything you do.

To understand the Alexander principle, and the Technique that derives from it, however, we need to learn more about Alexander himself and how he made his great discovery. "This story of perceptiveness, of intelligence and of persistence, shown by a man without medical training," said Professor Tinbergen in his Nobel speech, "is one of the true epics of medical research and practice."

# II
# *How the Technique Was Discovered*

M any a major innovation in the history of science appears to have been lying there, just waiting for the great person who discovered it. In this way, Newton and Leibniz, acting independently of one another, are said to have hit upon the powerful mathematical tool of calculus at about the same moment in history.

But there are other turning points, no less significant for the welfare of the human race, that have been reached in total isolation from any ongoing tradition of study and research. At first glance, the new proposition put forth appears to have sprung full-blown from the brain of its originator. And upon closer inspection, we can see that it does indeed owe almost everything to the peculiar genius of that individual and to the special circumstances of his or her particular life. This is certainly true of the way the Alexander Technique was discovered.

## The Australian Story

Frederick Matthias Alexander came from a remote outpost of the Australian bush country. He was born in 1869 on the island of Tasmania in a small town named Wynyard. Not much is known about his father except that he was poor and hard-working. Whatever influence he may have had on his son was far overshadowed by the boy's mother, an unusual woman who was close to the child during his formative years. In this wild and remote part of the world, she combined two of her talents, riding and midwifery (which included nursing and other medical services) to help her neighbors. Local doctors often called on her, and sometimes in response to urgent calls, she had been known to saddle her horse and leap it over the paddock gate so as not to lose time fooling with the latch.

From the beginning, Alexander was different from other children. He seemed to have an innate distrust of accepted routine and conventional wisdom, refusing to accept anything on blind faith. Fortunately, his schoolmaster, a Scot who had emigrated to Australia in an effort to repair his health, saw that his difficult pupil was something more than the usual rebellious student. He persuaded Alexander's father to let him tutor the boy in the evenings, which was all the formal education the youngster received. Thus, tutored but not formally taught, Alexander won prizes and passed examinations with ease.

## Crisis on Stage

He could have become the teacher his tutor wanted him to be, but family poverty demanded that the

eldest son go out to work, so he took a job with the
local tin mining company. He would have liked to go
on the stage, for the theater had been his love since
early childhood, when he began at six to practice the
kind of recitations so popular in that day. By the time
he was nineteen, Alexander was already considered
an accomplished reciter of Shakespeare, and away
from the mining company could consider himself
legitimately to be a professional actor, giving his recitals on numerous small-town stages. After the mining
came a succession of other uncongenial positions. In
Melbourne, finally, trying to recoup his small fortune
with odd jobs, he decided to cast his lot with the
theater as actor, recitalist or both.

He worked under a handicap, however, and it was
this disability which proved to be the determining factor in his life. Sometimes during recitals his voice failed
him completely—disturbing enough for any actor! Doctors could give him no more than temporary relief.
Meanwhile, the condition gradually worsened until he
finally had to refuse engagements if he thought he
might be incapable of getting through the performance. One night, halfway through an important engagement during the 1888 season, he lost his voice and
left the stage in near despair.

## The Patient Scientist

That was the turning point. There were to be no more
doctors. Instead, Alexander began to examine closely
how he used himself physically when he was on stage—
keeping his eyes open and observing, which is fundamental to the spirit of all scientific inquiry.

This close scrutiny continued for nearly ten years. At

first, Alexander devoted himself to finding out what made him lose his voice, using mirrors while he declaimed as an aid to observation. Soon he began to go beyond his immediate problem, becoming fascinated with the whole question of what happens to the body not only in speech, but also during any physical activity. In time, he came upon the characteristic that was blocking his own activity. He discovered that every movement he made was accompanied by a slight tendency to tighten the back of his neck and pull his head backward and down. This was something he did, not only during his stage appearances, but also when speaking normally in ordinary conversation.

Changing the poise of his head by pulling it backward and down was, in fact, part of a whole body pattern that also included lifting his chest and hollowing his back. This pattern of unconscious activity constituted the preliminary to every recitation he gave. Once aware of it, he could see the same pattern at work as involuntary preparation in whatever else he undertook, quite apart from speaking. In everyday physical acts, from the most trivial to the most strenuous, he began with that slight pulling backward and down of his head. It was only more noticeable in formal recitation because there it produced a depression of the larynx and an audible sucking in of his breath that could, with attention, be seen and heard. He observed similar consequences, on a different scale, in everything else he did; all his other activities were likewise initiated in the same self-stultifying manner.

## A Unique Mission

Since these patterns of bad use were triggered by an unconscious reflex of pulling the head backward and down, the obvious solution was to allow the neck to be free and the head to move forward and upward from its down-back position, thus eliminating the negative effects of bad use.

Thus, after he had completely corrected the long-standing vocal disability that drove him from the stage, Alexander resumed his theatrical career. But not for long. For as he pondered the far-reaching consequences of his startling discovery for the physical, mental and emotional well-being of people everywhere, no matter what business or occupation, he withdrew more and more from acting, finally abandoning the stage to carve a unique career as a teacher of the Alexander Technique. He continued this mission until his death at the age of eighty-six. Statesmen, industrialists, theater people, writers, diplomats, movie stars, athletes and celebrities of all kinds sought him out, and during his lifetime he worked both in England and America. Through his students, his teachings spread to Denmark, Israel, France, Switzerland, Italy, Australia, New Zealand, South Africa and other countries of the world. He also produced several books, and a valuable compilation of his basic writings may be found in *The Alexander Technique: The Essential Writings of F. Matthias Alexander*, edited by Edward Maisel.

## The Search and the Answer

We can come closer to understanding the nature of the discovery that underlies all we are going to learn in book if we now outline it in the terms suggested at the outset of this chapter: a special kind of person makes an important finding through the circumstances of his or her particular life and in isolation from any tradition of scientific thought on the subject.

The scene is Australia during the 1880s, where we find the young Alexander confronted with a problem of survival. His great love for the theater had caused him to gravitate through a series of unchallenging occupations before attaining, at last, a career on the stage.

At the age of nineteen, he is an actor specializing in the recital of long passages from the works of classic playwrights. His career seems assured—his reputation is growing steadily, and his only stumbling block is the occasional but very annoying tendency of his voice to give out during recitals.

Eventually, he is forced to see a doctor about the problem. It turns out that the doctor cannot find the cause, but he does prescribe a medicine that might just do the trick.

Thus armed, Alexander resumes his profession with renewed confidence, only to have his voice fail completely halfway through an especially important engagement.

No use in seeing more and more doctors, for he realizes that the physicians of his day know even less about his condition than he does. This leaves him with the ugly choice between (1) leaving the theater altogether or (2) applying himself tirelessly to discovering the cause of the problem. Being a far from submissive personality, Alexander chooses the latter.

While carefully limiting his theatrical obligations, he devotes the rest of his time to a painstaking and meticulous observation of the only clue he has—himself.

Through years of carefully watching his every motion in an elaborate system of mirrors, results are frustratingly slow in coming. In fact, it takes almost ten years of searching through more minute movements before the secret reveals itself.

That secret is a small but perceptible contraction of the muscles at the back of his neck, and it precedes all efforts at vocal articulation. Alexander has found the key; a remedy will follow. He must release that contraction and allow his head to move forward and upward.

## Outwitting Our Destructive Habits

Basically, the action that most often precedes wasteful or harmful responses is a contraction which pulls the head slightly backward and down. The effect of this is a compression of the spine, which, repeated hundreds of times a day over a span of many years, interferes with the smooth operation of the muscular and nervous systems and all the vital organs.

And this is only *one* destructive habit, the first of a whole series that will follow if the first occurs unchallenged. Taken together, this destructive series can compress the body's trunk, thus squeezing the delicate organs that reside there, reducing lung capacity and projecting the stomach unpleasingly forward. It can lead to round-the-clock tension in some muscles, which can cause loss of voice, high blood pressure and chronic joint and muscle pains.

To eliminate the problem at its source, we need to prevent the neck from contracting unnecessarily. And doing this means using the conscious mind to change our *sub*conscious muscle patterns. In order to revise things of which we are not aware, we need a new approach—one that can bring subconscious sensations forward into the conscious mind. With every act, we can consciously allow our head to move upward, body following it.

## Those Puritanical Hang-Ups

A major conclusion that emerged from Alexander's study and observation, and from his later teaching experience, was this: mind and body are inextricably bound together. They form an inseparable whole. The person is one psychophysical organism. We are not split into body and mind.

Unfortunately, the customs of language entrap us much of the time into thinking so. "A sound mind in a sound body," we glibly say, quoting the ancient Greeks, at the same time visualizing a something mental that is embedded in a something fleshly. Often, if we happen to suffer from puritanical hang-ups, we tend to look down upon the fleshly part as being inferior, in fact downright lowly, compared to the mind, or higher part. With disastrous consequences for our daily life, we may even persist in believing that the physical business of daily existence is unimportant or at least unworthy of our serious attention. The leaves go unraked, the clutter of papers on the desk remains untidy, the garbage is not carried out, the kitchen mess accumulates, personal grooming is neglected or forgotten...Disdain for the mere "physical," thus mistakenly conceived, can manifest itself in any of a thousand different ways that upset or swamp us.

Whenever we divide ourselves in two like this, into a mental part and a physical part, we also run the risk of never being rid of our troubles. After all, the fault lies with one of those two separate halves. It's "that damn leg of mine." Or "my thoughts keep wandering." We have something to blame. Instead, we could be finding out what we are doing to ourselves that keeps us from solving our problems.

# III

# *Bringing the Alexander Technique into Your Life*

Taking Alexander's discovery into your own life can mean strength, ease and endurance in everything you do—even sleeping. Besides, the effects can afford relief in a very wide range of ailments that are caused, directly or indirectly, by stress and excess muscle tension.

Adopting the Technique does not require you to embrace a new religion or far-out philosophy. It simply offers a different biological approach from the one you have been using, a new way to integrate thought with action.

Sir Charles S. Sherrington, the great Nobel Prize physiologist, once praised Alexander for his discovery. "To take a step is an affair not of this or that limb solely," he wrote, "but the total neuromuscular activity of the moment." The Australian was therefore correct, he said, in insisting upon "treating each act as involving the whole integrated individual, the whole psychophysical man."

We can readily see why, for everything we do, casual

or major, always involves us in patterns of movement and rest. It does not matter *what* the activity is: lying in bed, standing up, sitting down, opening and shutting doors, walking, getting in and out of automobiles, closing windows, reaching to a shelf, writing with a pen or pencil, unscrewing the caps of jars or uncorking bottles. However we go through any or all these activities, our particular patterns of movement and rest constitute the particular use (Alexander's word) that we make of ourselves.

## What Is Good Use?

The key concept of "use" is perhaps the easiest way to explain the Alexander Technique. Good use means moving the body with maximum balance and coordination of all parts so that only the effort absolutely needed is expended. Bad use means employing the body in a haphazard way: one part of the body compensates at random, and usually inefficiently, for the movement of another in order to maintain balance and stability. Good or bad, however, everything we do in life manifests itself in the way we "use" ourselves.

When your body is erect, it provides enough room for your organs so that your breath can massage them. If you are slumped down, you're putting unnecessary pressure on the organs so that they can't function as well. Circulation is slowed down. It's the same thing with your spine; for unless the vertebrae are stacked evenly, the pressure of the body being supported by them is not evenly shared. Some parts of the spinal cord will then experience more pressure than others. Sometimes nerves are pinched, and that causes malfunctioning of the parts of the body serviced by them.

If you try simply to push yourself erect, the only possible result is that while you may be lengthening some muscles, you will be shortening others drastically. So in this attempt to gain desirable results forcibly, you simply abuse yourself in another manner. It sometimes happens that when you experience pain anywhere, as from a twisted ankle, arthritic joints or an upset stomach, you unconsciously tighten the painful area and often other parts of the body as well. You do so presumably to protect the injured area by immobilizing it, but in fact this new excess tension in the joints and muscles will slow down circulation and actually prevent your body from healing itself.

Indeed, whenever you move without awareness, these conditions of excessive muscular tension are likely to exist. The object is not to learn all the proper combinations of muscular action needed for all that you do and then try to think of them constantly as you move. Such a course is both impossible and unnecessary. Through the Alexander Technique, you learn instead one Basic Movement that can control the normal flow of all your activity. The aim of the Technique is to allow a condition of ease throughout the body without creating any new distortions in the process.

## You Are Not a Statue

Making good use of yourself by means of the Technique must never be equated with the static thing known as "posture," a word that ought to be jettisoned because it in no way corresponds to the conditions of real life. Conceivably, the word might apply on the rare occasions when you take a stance before coming into a room, or when you stand poised at the head of the stairs. Once you have entered the room, however, or the very moment you start descending the stairs, you are again caught up in movement. And your customary use of yourself will reappear immediately, since its absence was based on nothing more than that transient "holding-in" known as posture.

So in learning the Alexander Technique, you must at the outset dismiss from your mind all shining examples of good posture. Forget the paragons of close-order drill in the Marine Corps or the symmetrical ranks of the chorus line at the Folies Bergère. For when they depart the parade grounds or the music hall, leathernecks and chorines alike let go of these strenuously maintained body attitudes. In the ordinary work of walking and living, they drop the elevated chest and the forward curvature of the spine, with its accompanying hollow in the back. The effort to hang on to some deliberate position, no matter what kind, is continuous and involves both physical and mental fatigue.

It is in fact quite absurd to think of attaining some ideal posture and then clinging to it through all your subsequent activity. You are not a statue to be propped about in various juxtapositions to meet the changing requirements of whatever you are engaged in. Unfortunately, though, there are people who do indeed seem to be trying to preserve just such a rigid and invariant attitude through all that they do.

## No Positions, No Poses

To forestall any possibility of error, to prevent the least trace of confusion, it may be well to state flatly what the Alexander Technique is *not*. You will *not* be asked to memorize the "right" pose for every possible body position (sitting, standing and so on) and then go through life using these and only these poses. First of all, the mere act of getting out of a chair takes the body through more than a hundred positions; the positions involved in darning a sock would require a whole lifetime of memorization. Second, there is no "right" pose for any position, and even if there were, it would be different for every person on this planet because each human body is different.

## How to Look at The Pictures

When you consult the photos that accompany the directions in this book, do not look upon them as static poses or positions to be imitated. Think of them as having been extracted from some ongoing movement. They are intended only as a guide or pointer to the action described. Ideally, each illustration should be provided by stroboscopic photography or some other form of action picture. However, the blurry effects of such an attempt at authenticity would nullify the purposes of useful and simple instruction.

## The Breath of Life

A vital function of our body that is impaired by bad use is breathing. If you slump even slightly, your lung capacity is thereby diminished. This forces you to breathe with your upper chest rather than with your lower ribs and diaphragm. When you are not slumped, more room is provided in the chest cavity. More air can then pass in and out of the lungs, and, as a result, more waste materials are cleansed from your body. With the increase in the freedom of your breathing machinery, the quality of your voice can improve.

## Let It Happen

Good breathing is integral to the Alexander Technique. This does not mean that you will need to practice it in the form of separate and isolated breathing exercises. As you begin to correct your faulty use, excess muscular tension will disappear. With the release of that tension, the action of your ribs and diaphragm in breathing will automatically take care of itself.

As you progress, you may find yourself yawning or emitting deep sighs. Let them happen, for they come involuntarily and are an excellent sign that you are getting rid of excess tension. You will find that breathing supports movement at the same time that movement supports breathing. This natural and inevitable orchestration of the two is very different from superimposing some artificially learned breathing pattern upon your movements. Make sure you don't hold your breath. Don't try to do anything. Let it happen.

## Your Breathing Improves

Notice, when talking, whether you are breathing in through your nose or your mouth. Give yourself time to breathe. It is helpful on occasion to close your lips and allow the air to come in through your nose when you need breath. This helps to release any tightness in the throat.

Many of us develop the habit of gulping or sucking in air which tenses the throat and is accompanied by a downward pull of the head. If you don't collapse and pull down at the end of the out-going breath, a slight vacuum is created in the lungs which pulls in the air for you. When you breathe normally in this way, every time stale air leaves your lungs, new air will automatically come back in. Through the Alexander Technique, you can learn to leave your breathing mechanism—your body—alone to function freely and without effort.

## How We Got This Way

To be sure, in this misguided quest, the breathing-exercisers and the posture-builders may really be seeking some of the benefits that are achieved by the Alexander Technique. The grace and naturalness that the Technique imparts to you will be highly noticeable. Whenever you use it, your entire body will be more erect—your chest is not collapsed, your torso does not settle in on itself. As you continue to practice, an improvement in muscle tone occurs.

If such are the blessings reaped through making good use of oneself, why are they so deplorably lacking in most of us? What has gone wrong? Why so much grief physically and mentally?

It is the burden of civilization's advance, Alexander believed, that has brought upon us our present deterio-rated condition. Today, instead of adapting our bodies to a slowly changing terrain, we capriciously adapt a fast-changing environment to arbitrary standards of comfort (even taste). Through current upheaval, the one thing that has remained essentially the same is the structure of the human body.

Prior to the development of technology, changes in the world around us took place over a span of millions of years, slow enough for us to keep pace through subtle, unconscious alterations in the body itself. But our restless civilization has brought about a revolution in our surroundings so rapid that this process of gradual development has been quite outdistanced. As a result, the world we know now is completely foreign to the one to which human beings long ago adjusted.

Our life-style has become a hybrid interaction of a body, originally adapted to primitive survival, with an environment of elevators, mattresses, automobiles and comfy chairs. Our physical and social universe is radically different, and our physical equipment has been impaired in its responses to the new demands thrust upon it by contemporary living. We have to make intelligent use of ourselves, said Alexander, if we want to meet the new conditions effectively.

## Three Easy Tests

To illustrate the degenerative influence that civilized living has exerted upon the human organism, Alexander proposed three simple tests: (You are requested to interrupt your reading for a moment and carry out the following three experiments.)

1. Move your head without your shoulders.
2. Open your mouth without tilting your head back.
3. Turn out your toes without first shifting your heels.

While doing each test, be alert and sensitive in registering how you move so you may catch the unnecessary movement involved.

## See for Yourself

In quite the same spirit of experiment, you may now begin to notice, in the course of your daily activity, how you go about handling objects.

Next time you brush your teeth, for example, stay alert and observe just how heavy the toothbrush is, how much energy is required to lift it and keep it in your hand. How much pressure is needed to brush? In the toothpaste commercials on television, it sometimes appears as though the people are trying to brush the teeth right out of their mouths. (See Fig. 8, p. 83.)

You can make similar observations when you sit down to write a letter. With a little try-and-see, you can tell how much strength is actually required to hold onto the pen and get the ink to flow onto the paper.

Once you consider how you actually go through any activity, you can begin to affect a change in your performance of it.

## The Road to Take

Animals in the wild miss out on the satisfactions, cultural advantages and triumphs of civilization, but they are likewise spared its debilitating side effects. They have no price to pay. In a famous allegory, the German writer Heinrich von Kleist makes this point by describing how a chained bear, relying on animal instinct, successfully defends itself by exerting very slight movements to deflect the thrusts and feints of a champion swordsman. The human antagonist is baffled by the perfect efficiency of the beast's innate responses.

Observe even a domestic animal, like a cat or a dog, at rest, and you will see a creature completely relaxed yet still capable of making sudden, definite movements. What is more, the expenditure of energy in animal movement is exquisitely attuned to the requirements of what needs to be done. No overdoing; no underdoing.

But the answer to the perilous misfunction that has befallen mankind through the anxiety and stress of modern living cannot be to call a halt to civilization. We are not about to rejoin the lower animals or "go primitive." There is, however, a sane solution to our problem.

In curing himself of his loss of voice by noting the slight pulling backward and down of his head, which accompanied formal recitation, Alexander uncovered the whole pattern of bad use. It is this same harmful pattern of involuntary preparation which is involved in everything we do. And it is this, more than anything else, which blocks, prevents, defeats and frustrates whatever we may intend on every level of our existence— physical, emotional and mental.

The road to the recuperation of our diminished faculties, which we will learn in this book, and which is the essence of the Alexander Technique, may be enunciated as follows: *as you begin any movement or act, allow your whole head to move forward and upward and away from your whole body, and let your whole body follow that upward direction by lengthening.*

# IV
# *The Basic Movement*

You are now ready to learn the Basic Movement that incorporates the Alexander principle in a form you can practice whenever you wish.

The mere performance of this simple movement can, if you extend it through the whole range of your normal activity, put you on the road to a new life of health, physical freedom and, in the deepest sense, personal happiness.

## Not an Exercise

But first a word about a word. The word "movement" as used here has nothing to do with the 1-2-3-4! 1-2-3-4! fitness exercises you did in gym class. It is in no way related to muscle-snapping, joint-wrenching gyrations of any kind.

In the Basic Movement, and everywhere else in this book where a movement or action is given, the word always refers to some movement or action of the utmost simplicity. You are not called upon to run miles or to lift heavy weights. There are no exercises in this book. Nothing tiresome will be required of you.

This distinction is especially important because, as we shall see in the following chapter, the typical physical fitness approach stands in direct opposition to the Alexander Technique. It is true, however, that the strenuous and repetitive exertions popularly known as "aerobics" can be performed more effectively and with much greater benefit once you learn the Basic Movement and apply its principle to them.

The same applies to those more skilled and motivated forms of physical exercise which we call sports. Whether you play golf or tennis, swim or bowl, or whatever your game may be, it can undergo amazing improvement after you have bettered the use of your body in pursuing it. Some Olympic rowers, for example, have learned the Alexander Technique because it makes a real difference in crew performance.


## How to Start

The Basic Movement is preceded by a brief inspection of your total condition while you carry out the action in your customary or habitual manner. This moment of self-observation is presented under the heading "Exploring Yourself," and the same format is used as a preliminary to every other movement or action in this book.

Next follow the instructions for the Basic Movement itself. It is not to be repeated mindlessly in hopes of programming yourself into some automatic routine that has nothing directly to do with daily living. It provides, rather, a guideline to follow: a new way of thinking and

moving. The sooner you apply to any normal activity—
such as tying your shoe or lifting a bag of groceries—
the Basic Movement of *letting your head move forward and
up and letting your body follow,* the sooner you will experience a new lightness and ease and a sense of real
assurance in whatever you may be doing.

# The Basic Movement

## Exploring Yourself

You may carry out this movement either while seated or
standing. We shall do it sitting.

Turn your head to look around you. No trance: eyes
open. See the room. Tip your head to look up at the
ceiling; then tip it down to look at the floor. Turn it
from side to side.

What do you notice about the turning of your head?
Do you feel any tense or tight muscles in your neck?
Does your body twist about when you turn your head? Do
you hear any popping, crackling sounds in your spine?
Is your breathing slowed or stopped?

## The Basic Movement

While turning your head slowly from one side to the
other in order to survey the room, add the Basic
Movement: allow your whole head to move forward
and upward and let your whole body follow. (Figs.
1, 2, 3.) Remember to keep your eyes open and *looking*.

Continue to allow *your whole head to move up and away
from your body* while you perform the turning move-

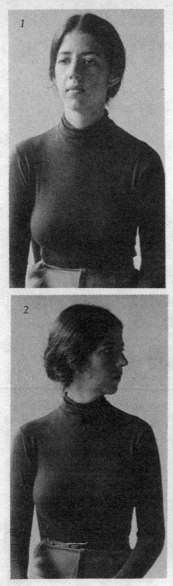

1. *Beginning from a usual slump.*

2. *Easing upward and away as you turn your head.*

3. *From side to side.*

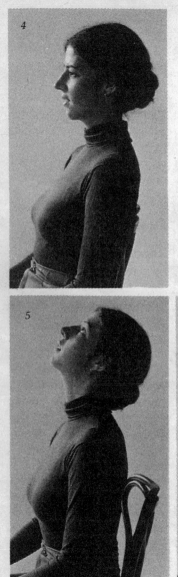

4. *Easing upward.*
5. *As you tip your head back.*
6. *And tip it forward.*

ment, so that your neck lengthens above your shoulders instead of craning forward or jamming back.

Notice if this upward direction of your head affects the smoothness and ease of the side-to-side motion. Notice if it brings up and aligns your body.

*Allow your whole body to follow the upward direction of your head.* This does not mean that your body twists and turns with your head, but that it is allowed to delicately lengthen without narrowing during your head movement.

Next, continuing to let your head ease up, tip it back to look up at the ceiling, then forward to look down at the floor. (Figs. 4, 5, 6.) The upward direction will keep you from cramping your neck throughout these movements. (Figs. 7, 8.)

*7, 8. Cramping your neck unnecessarily.*

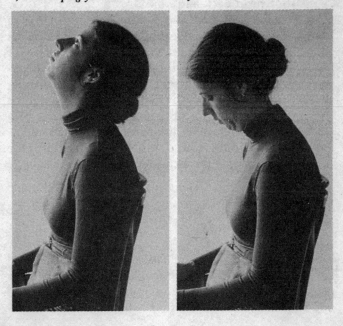

Now that you've gone through the Basic Movement once, the following clarification of the main words used should give you even more success the next time you do it.

## Your Whole Head

You must learn to think of your head as three-dimensional. When you are directed to move your head, this means your whole head, including the back, sides, top and front (your face). (Fig. 9.) Often people have a tendency to lead movements with their chin. (Fig. 10.) When you remember that your chin is part of your head, you will be less likely to jut it forward, which pulls your head back and down.

It is important that you realize how substantial a support your neck provides for your head. The fact is that the spine in your neck is very near the center of your neck, not just along the back of it as many imagine. Actually the top of your spine is located directly between your ears. Also, the diameter of your vertebrae is larger than that of a silver dollar—not the size of a nickel or a quarter. With this in mind, you will understand that you do not need to hold your head up; the neck is sturdy and the head rests easily on that large base as it moves.

## Your Whole Body

"Body" refers to your whole torso. It begins at the base of your neck, includes your shoulders and ends at your hip joints, the bottom line of your buttocks. (Fig. 11.) Remember to think of your whole body as three-

9. *The whole head.*

10. *Jutting the chin forward
    needlessly.*

## 11. The whole body.

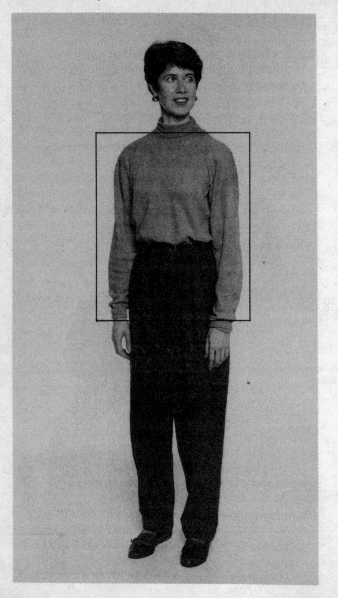

dimensional, including sides, back and front, in following the instructions. People tend to think of only one dimension when allowing their body to move upward: either their front or their back. As a result, their body will curve forward or backward, causing unnecessary effort. Your entire torso must be considered and no part forgotten.

## The Upward Direction

"Upward" does not necessarily mean ceilingward. It means the moving of your head up and away from your body, and the moving of your torso up from the hips. When you are sitting or standing, that direction is, of course, up toward the ceiling. (Fig. 12.) However, as you lean your body to the side, "upward" is where the top of your spine points. (Fig. 13.) Above all, remember that upward always applies to movement—wherever the top of the spine happens to be pointing—and is not a fixed position. Upward directs a positive action in order to prevent the usual negative action of pulling the head back and down and slumping. We're aiming for as much flexibility and ease as possible.

Because your torso is connected to your head, when you allow your head to move upward, your body must follow. Simple as this may seem, you must not forget it. If you remember this connection, you will find that your body will automatically want to follow that upward movement.

## Forward

At the same time the head is moving up it can delicately rotate forward. This forward rotation is the tiniest of movements and it should not cause you to tuck your chin into your throat or push your head in front of your body. Think of the motion taking place at the top of the spine, right between your ears, rather than at your chin. In figure 10 the head is going in a back and down direction. As you look at the picture again think of what the opposite direction to back and down would

*12. Upward*

be and you'll have a clear idea of the forward and upward direction.

## Lengthening

As your whole body follows the upward direction of your head it will naturally lengthen upward. However, do not mistakenly think that while your body gets longer it has to get narrower. A greater benefit will be derived from allowing your torso to release gently outward, letting your sides release wide, your back release back and your upper chest softly expand. So

*13. Upward*

while your body follows the upward direction of your head it lengthens *and* widens.

## On Your Way

Repeat the Basic Movement and see what happens. You will probably experience some sort of change or notice some difference. Perhaps you'll be aware that you were pushing yourself and using more effort to sit (or stand) than you are now. Or maybe you'll feel that it is easier to move your head in the way described. In any case, you will have begun the process of keeping your eyes open and observing how you move.

## The Instant Train

The movement of the body following the head is fundamental to the Alexander Technique. You might compare it to the image of a train. The engine represents the head, and the cars the remainder of the body. If it is linked up properly, there will be no time lag between the movement of the cars and engine. Although the engine always begins the movement of the train, its forward impetus is transmitted almost simultaneously to each car behind. Or as Alexander once paradoxically described the movement: "All together one after another."

## How to Succeed Without Really Trying

Most people learning something new are eager to discover the "right" way to do it. Here, though, you are not required to take up any new position in order to correct your misuse. For as we have seen in the preceding chapter, there are no "right" positions. What matters is that you improve the process of *how* you move.

The Basic Movement is a first-class example of the way a very simple adjustment in the use we make of ourselves can have tremendous, far-reaching consequences. It is a single adjustment, a very subtle and *continuous* movement of the head upward "only an infinitesimal amount" (as Alexander wrote from England to a man in America who was learning the Technique on his own).

The Basic Movement is accomplished without any big, obvious, external show. The movement of your head is tiny, on the order of millimeters. However, some people are reluctant to believe that anything remarkable can result from the Alexander Technique unless they do something that demonstrates huge effort. They strain their necks mightily; they try to become human giraffes. *But no neck-stretching whatever is required!* All that is really necessary is to use your thinking. Studies in sports psychology have shown that every thought we have creates a corresponding muscular response, however slight. Think of your whole head moving delicately forward and upward and your body following it and you will create the powerful, infinitesimal change we are after.

It is perhaps part of our American credo to believe that only prodigious feats can produce worthwhile results. Here, though, is one case where the big results come from a tiny change. The new science of chaos describes the butterfly effect, where it is possible that a movement as tiny as a butterfly flapping its wings in Brazil may ultimately cause a dramatic change in the

outcome of weather in Nebraska. And so it is with the
Alexander Technique: your ruler may not detect the
difference but you will feel it in every bone in your
body.

# V

# *Become a Whole Person*

The Basic Movement you have just learned, and the seven supplementary Actions that will follow in Part II, are clearly of a very different order from the strenuous push-pull, up-down, left-right activity most of us associate with physical fitness. This is because they have been designed with a very different objective from that of ordinary aerobics.

## The Trouble with Physical Exercises

After visiting the gym of a leading exercise teacher in Australia one day, Alexander became convinced that such training would never meet the needs of people who came there in quest of physical development. If they used themselves badly in ordinary life, they would continue to do so throughout their physical exertions. In fact, the repeated and accentuated performance of the prescribed movements—thus badly executed—increased the damage they were already doing themselves.

"There was a crooked man," the well-known nursery rhyme tells us, "and he walked a crooked mile." Just so. If we comport ourselves in a manner that is harmful, any exercises we do to get in shape will likewise be carried out in a manner that is harmful. While they may improve our cardiovascular condition, the stress and strain we experience in daily life is not likely to change for the better.

Much the same is true of the numerous varieties of physical manipulation and massage that are applied to our bodies. Some of these bestow considerable good upon us, but their intention is not to teach a better use of ourselves. Perhaps a golfer can find, through alleviating treatment of this kind, some welcome temporary relief from the pains and aches caused by a faulty swing, but his trouble will surely recur if the error in his swing is not corrected.

## The Trance in Which We Live

Unlike conventional exercise and manipulation, the Alexander Technique coordinates conscious thought with action in order that you may deal with yourself. Most of the time we operate our bodies on a subconscious level. We unfold the whole repertoire of our daily activity with little attention to *how* we are doing what we are doing. Consider, for example, driving a car. How often have you driven from point A to point B without noticing what lies between or even how you got to point B. Or again, if you are accustomed to a standard shift, think back to the last time you borrowed an automatic car and reached down for gears that weren't there.

In this half-conscious state in which we operate, we pay scant heed to the constant flow of information that is being communicated by our bodies. Only the very gross or screaming message—a headache, a muscle cramp, sore ligaments or illness—gets through. We continue wearing ourselves out and tearing ourselves apart from day to day because we remain in deep ignorance of our bad tension habits until we reach a crisis of pain or run into some drastic physical or emotional trouble.

Moreover, as these bad habits have developed little by little, so too has our sensory awareness gradually adjusted to them. We cannot perceive the faulty way we are using ourselves because it has come to "feel right." We simply don't get true messages from our bodies anymore. Thus, a person may carry one shoulder higher than the other and never notice (were his shoulders to be set level for him, they would now feel "wrong," ludicrously askew). Another person may be oblivious to a tendency to lift her chin and jut it forward (until she sees herself on television).

## Our Mistaken Ideas About Ourselves

There is still another factor at work in this universal unfamiliarity with ourselves and our functioning. Perhaps no one has given a sharper and more disquieting picture of it than the writer Arthur Koestler. People who listen for the first time to the sound of their voice played back on a tape recorder usually get a shock, says Koestler. He offers himself as an example: "I am of Hungarian origin, and although my foreign accent retains the specific density of pea-soup, I was virtually unaware of this till I first listened to my voice on a recorded broadcast. I have a good ear for other people's accents, yet perceive my own voice as if it were free from it." So too may our singing be stridently out of tune and yet sound just fine to us until a musical accompaniment pulls us back on the track.

All this occurs, according to Koestler, because in the perception of one's own voice, the actual acoustic production plays a subordinate part. The main component of what we perceive is the sound we think we are projecting. There may be a world of difference between what we think we hear and our performance as heard by others, but this discrepancy is masked from us by the process of hearing what we intend and not what we are in fact uttering.

The same applies also to our gestures and movements, however defective and self-defeating they may be, remarks Koestler. "The clumsy gesture is screened off from awareness by the direct impact of the image of the intended graceful movement on perception."

## The Crown of the Senses

So how do we defeat this tendency toward what might be called a kind of wish-fulfillment in our senses, caused by a confusion between the event as intended and the event as it really happens? How, in short, do we get rid of the bad habits that plague us?'

The Alexander Technique, and, therefore, all the Actions in this book for learning it, meets the problem by calling upon a faculty we all possess but often overlook because it is not one of the so-called "five senses" we usually talk about. It is not one of the original five long ago listed by Aristotle, but in calling upon this faculty, a real chance is offered for the enrichment of our entire organism.

This enricher of the whole person is considered by some connoisseurs and gourmets of good physical condition to be nothing less than "the crown of the senses," the distinguishing mark of superb physical condition. Whenever we admire the seemingly effortless coordination in the movements of a great athlete, or the agile ease and poise of a friend in the way he handles himself in all the ordinary activities of life, we are paying tribute to it.

Clearly evident in people like circus aerialists, jugglers or sculptors, it is deplorably lacking in a very great number of us. At the UNESCO conference on brain mechanisms and awareness, one speaker even accused the others, in their concern with it, of trying to "unscrew the inscrutable."

It is not really that inscrutable. Most everyone knows something at least about this faculty, or the "kinesthetic sense" as it is called. It is sometimes called the "muscle sense," though actually its sense organs may be found not only in the muscles, but in the tendons and joint membranes as well. It is by means of this sense that we remain aware of the position of every part of our body even when our eyes are closed. It is from this sense that we are continually receiving knowledge of the gestures we make and of the pressures or tensions anywhere in our body. We use it to assess the range and force of our movements and also in adapting ourselves to the weight of anything we lift.

"Kinesthetic" is a cross between the words "kinetic" (motion) and "esthetic" (feeling) and means "feeling motion." Since it is essential in the practice of the Alexander Technique, the development of this sense underlies the entire program set forth in this book. In order to ensure that we are using our bodies properly, we do not have to know the names of our muscles or how to locate them on a chart. It is the kinesthetic sense that supplies the information we need. We can feel what we are doing and, in this way, get a good, clear idea of ourselves in action.

Through the sensitive practice of the Basic Movement and the seven Actions which build upon it, we can increase the reliability of our kinesthetic sense and establish a new standard of good use.

## Discover a World Within

The "crown of the senses," heralded by Alexander, has come very much to the foreground in the U.S. during the past decade due to the popular rise of the human potential movement. Virtually every branch of that movement makes some use of body awareness. It was, however, by no means entirely forgotten in earlier American efforts to promote physical and emotional fitness. The wise and respected new England medical educator Dr. George V. N. Dearborn always emphasized the important place that the kinesthetic sense holds in the life of every human being. He called it "the warp of the sensation-fabric—the personality's dynamic index of its body."

One trouble, as Dr. Dearborn pointed out, is that the much stronger sense experiences of light and color may drown out this subtler experience, sometimes so completely that many intelligent people go through their days "wholly ignorant even of the essential existence of these warp-threads in the fabric of our conscious life."

The effective practice of the Alexander Technique

makes it possible to receive increasingly subtle messages from within. This in turn produces a harmonious interplay of all our faculties and thereby brings about the first visible fruit of our growing kinesthetic development: good muscular coordination.

## Part Person vs. Whole Person

There are always two ways a person can learn to carry out any action. One way is to focus on the single part of the body that actually does the work. The other way is to use the natural integrating mechanism of the *whole* body, *all* parts included and coordinated to perform the action. This means using the principles in the Basic Movement.

With the first method, any number of things can happen that will cause more effort than necessary. For example, a person wanting to throw a ball will find that he must swing his arm. So he swings his arm as best he can. Because there are so many possible combinations of tension, he may unwittingly raise his shoulder. He has no real awareness of the rest of himself, and when he hoists his shoulder, his body may then compensate inefficiently to keep its balance.

The second way of performing an action is to involve your whole person in it. This does not mean exerting effort throughout your entire organism in order to swing your arm. Rather, you swing your arm in a manner that allows your whole body to be balanced and your energy to be directed effectively. It is the kinesthetic sense which, in time, enables you to allow this total pattern, the head moving delicately forward and upward and the body following, to control whatever you do.

## Staying in the Moment

In carrying out the Actions that follow, keep alert. Your eyes must not become glazed, but must see whatever they look at. Do not hold your breath from a sense of strain. From moment to moment, during the whole time you devote to an Action, be open to any and every message of feeling that comes to you from the various parts of your body. You will then discover for yourself what it means in actual practice, how it feels and how it affects a person to live by means of the unique, physically-mentally unified Technique you gain from these Actions. You will learn directly the benefits of this regular experience of complete personal harmony.

# VI
# *The Technique as a Way to Stay Young*

The youthful manner and attractive bearing attained through the Alexander Technique should dispel once and for all the conviction that men and women must inevitably bow down, stoop and wither before the onslaught of advancing years. Indeed, what used to be known as "dowager's hump," no longer related to income group or social status and every bit as typical of men as of women, is now surprisingly common at a much earlier time of life. An eyesore and a handicap, it has become a prevalent sign of our era.

We have all encountered at one time or another those rare men and women whose upright bearing, elastic lineaments, lithe movement and springy step belie their actual age. However, we tend to disregard or forget this reassuring evidence of our senses. We continue instead under the spell of the rather sinister and frightening idea, widely accepted at present, that the force of gravity, working against us through all the years of our life, pulls us down, down, down until finally, unequal to the combat, we are done in by it.

That gravity does indeed provide a persistent and unvarying element in man's ecology there can be no doubt. Like air, sunshine and other more familiar elements, it plays a major role in whatever we do. Since our body consists of mass, it is self-evident that all our movements and activities are subject to gravity's pull. That much is certainly true. But what about the rest of the theory?

## Why We Shrink

According to a popular view, we find ourselves inextricably locked in a lifelong struggle, pitting human strength against gravity's relentless power with no chance of winning. Throughout the day, without let-up or cease, it works its malign influence upon us. Studies have shown that between getting out of bed in the morning and getting back in at night, people actually lose about half an inch in height. During sleep, when we lie in a position parallel to the ground and thus alter the effects of the ubiquitous pull, we regain that lost stature. But the cumulative results of a lifetime of unequal struggle can be seen in some bent-over and hobbling older people who have lost many inches. Gravity has slowly squashed them to the ground.

The skylab astronauts gave us yet another glimpse of this force's baneful effects when they emerged—after months of living outside it—in a remarkably unkinked condition. They had even gained in height (and lost at the waist), which was partly the result of not being pulled down, as on earth, and thus being permitted to straighten out.

Down, down, down... The unflinching, unceasing pull upon us of this antagonistic force has been assigned responsibility for a very great number of the woes of aging. According to the biologist D'Arcy W. Thompson, it is felt "in every movement of our limbs, in every beat of our hearts," and "it leaves its mark in sagging wrinkles, drooping mouth and hanging breasts; it is the indomitable force which defeats us in the end, which lays us on our death bed and lowers us to the grave."

## The Upright Creature

Supposedly, all this is the price we pay for standing erect, and the problem is one that has been with us ever since the forepaws of our prehistoric ancestors left the ground. In this view, the quadruped is more fortunately constructed for resistance to gravity than we are. As bipeds, we seem peculiarly ill-equipped for maintaining an upright position. For one thing, we appear to be top-heavy, like an inverted pyramid, with our heavy head and shoulders weighing down the skeletal structure. Our spine is flexible, curved in several places, perhaps an ingenious device for cushioning shock, but far from ideal for steadying our weight. Physiologically, the weight of our inner organs is carried high above our center of gravity.

Standing or sitting, how—in this view—can we hope to contend with gravity's pull? We are compelled to oppose its force by sheer muscular power. Our structural frame is an intricate system of articulated levers—bones and joints—that are held and moved by our muscles and tendons. Just standing up is a kind of acrobatic triumph involving an exact balance of varying degrees of contraction and relaxation in more than two hundred pairs of muscles. These muscles are reflexively maintained in a state of tonus—partially contracted and ready for work—except when the body is lying completely horizontal.

## Must We Fall Apart?

While gravity depresses all the elements of the body, the greatest strain is sustained by the musculo-skeletal structure that keeps us erect. And strain means injury, deformation and distortion depending upon the disparity between the pull and each person's total power of response to it.

The immediate battleground for humans versus gravity may be discerned throughout the musculo-skeletal system whose mainstays are the pelvis, the spine and the network of muscles and ligaments. However, repercussions of the conflict are felt in all the other major systems of the body, in respiration and circulation as well as in the nervous system. Failure or defeat in any of these components adversely affects the overall struggle.

This situation is said to account for many of the chronic progressive and degenerative conditions which afflict the falteringly upright, two-legged human race. In a fierce book, *Mortal Lessons,* Dr. Richard Selzer totaled up the outward woes he thinks indicate that our erect stance cannot successfully resist the pressure imposed upon us by gravity. He found that body chemistry as well as the regulatory and coordination mechanisms of the body are all affected. According to Dr. Selzer, our vertebrae, piled one atop the other, slip, buckle and wear out. The arches of our feet fall. Our hip joints grind to a stop. Our flesh pushes itself through into hernias. Our blood gathers in hemorrhoids and varicose veins. Mental confusion, mood, feeling, attitude and behavior may also figure in the generalized failure of our adaptation to the ordinary strain of being on the earth's surface.

## How We Conquer

As it happens, the extreme and scary picture we have just looked at, which is so popular today, is both one-sided and incomplete. It does not fully or accurately represent man's complex relationship to the downward pull he experiences from the earth.

Man is a perfect match for gravity. In the very long history of walking erect, the human species, as Professor Tinbergen has pointed out, must have evolved a suitable equipment and the correct mechanism for biped locomotion. From an evolutionary viewpoint, the adventure of assuming an upright posture would probably never have been sustained if man had not become capable of it. We obviously had to develop a way of neutralizing the effects of gravity in order for our life to have continued on earth. And the mechanism is by now genetic. We inherit an easy good use of our bodies, which enables us to deal handily with the earth's pull.

This reflex of good use can be observed in infants. In the first two or three years of life as they gain mobility, and before they are physically corrupted, their actions are beautifully free and easy. They move in a superb manner quite naturally. Observe a baby come to sitting position by itself; the whole body is in a system of balance, no strain in the back or anywhere else. Or watch a baby turn its head; it pivots smoothly without tension.

## It Goes by Itself

Careful, detailed studies of this natural mechanism
have offered a technical explanation in anatomical and
physiological terms. In effect, what has been discovered
is that when all the body parts are balanced and integrated, the human species is constructed in a way to
resist the pull of gravity effortlessly in keeping itself
erect. When arranged naturally in a sort of flexible
column, with its energy and movement directed up
through the top of that column—the whole torso following the head—the body will work efficiently and
flexibly. (Fig. 1.) In this condition, the reflex system of
the body is allowed to work.

The correct messages from one body part to another
(coordination) are relayed and interpreted properly.
We no longer have to depend upon large jolts or shocks
from tensing muscles to tell us if something is happening. We sense a new way of moving, different from our
previous experience of tension-filled activity. Only those
muscles which are essential to a particular action are
used in that action. The movement of the head leads
and influences the movement of the body so that all
parts (muscles) are coordinated and work in a harmonious system of contraction and relaxation.

When we do not trust our body's ability and interfere
with this natural reflex of ease, things go wrong. If the
head does not initiate, the body column will be out of
kilter (Fig. 2.), the reflex of our movement will be
interfered with and muscle will be pitted against muscle. We actually feel heavier because of pressure put on
the joints by excess muscular tension.

In attempts to control ourselves, we shorten our

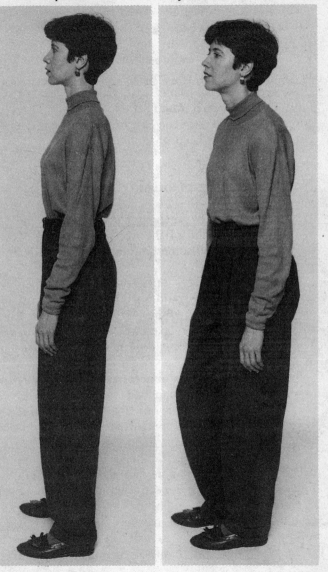

1. Energy and movement directed upward.

2. The body column out of kilter.

necks and pull our chests down, or shorten and arch
our backs. And it is because of these tense habits that it
so often feels as if gravity must be working against us.
Rather, it is *we* who work against ourselves, and gravity
merely compounds the problem. A jutting part here or
there creates an imbalance and, as with a leaning column or an uneven tower of blocks, some form of
additional support—in the case of the body, tense muscles—is needed to keep it standing.

## Never a Feeling of Strain

We meet gravity by keeping our "balance," and an
elementary definition of the word is: the state of not
having to hold onto something in order to maintain a
position.

Most of us consider ourselves balanced when we
stand (otherwise how could we?). But in fact we usually
are holding onto something—namely, ourselves. Even
when we think we're relaxed, muscles throughout the
body are tensing—holding on—in an effort to keep us
as we are.

Such excess tension is unnecessary. The magnificent
engineering of the human body does not require it.
Our bone structure (skeleton) is so finely organized a
system of arches and supports that it takes only a tiny
contraction of muscles to maintain us in the "work"
of standing. Bringing the head into real physical
balance on top of the spine and allowing the body to
follow, produces this desired alignment of the total
structure. The new equilibrium gives relief and freedom to dozens of muscles that were previously engaged
full time in "holding on" to maintain a condition that is
at best a rough and hapless approximation of true

balance. And this muscular release goes a long way toward explaining why the Technique is effective in eliminating superfluous tension.

## A Future Without Fear

Proper adjustment to gravity in the way we stand, walk and move, then, is obviously an old, inherited form of behavior. Our misuse of ourselves in all that we do is the consequence of modern living. Most of us are still trapped by the distant voices of parents and teachers repeating: "Stand up straight," "Don't slouch," "Your posture is terrible." Or "Little girls don't sit like that." But long before we heard these and similar unhelpful exhortations, our superb natural functioning had already vanished because of the way we were handled as infants, through the models we encountered and imitated in early family life and school, through the tasks we were called upon to perform before we had the physical capacity or readiness, and through our adaptation to the furniture and paraphernalia with which we lived.

This is why the popular picture of gravity as inescapable master and despoiler is for so many of us the stark truth. In the way we misuse ourselves, we violate our own natural mechanism for meeting the downward pull exerted on all forms of terrestrial life.

The foreshortening of the back neck muscles with which we initiate our every act, and which Alexander pinpointed as the root of our difficulties, means that tension and gravity are operating in concert. The effect is too strong for the body to resist, and the entire trunk and spine are slowly compressed.

But this need not be. By means of the Alexander

Technique, we can call a halt to our customary interference with the body's natural reflexes and thus facilitate our anti-gravity response. The upward movement of the head followed by the body can free us to initiate whatever *we* choose to do in whatever manner *we* choose to do it. We are no longer the helpless playthings or victims of a hostile force from below.

The youngster now starting out, or the adult of middle or advanced age, has no reason to dread that the years ahead are going to pull him or her down in a decline of slow surrender to gravity. We can reverse that trend once and for all the moment we decide to change our bad use of ourselves and reinstate our pristine grace. By means of the Alexander Technique, we can regain our easeful place on the planet and go confidently forward with the concerns that matter in our life.

# PART II

## *The Practice of the Technique*

### HOW TO DO IT

# The Seven Actions

## An Effortless Program

The following chapters present a simple step-by-step program of seven Actions for learning the Alexander Technique, which will show you how to apply the basic principle to all your movements.

Each step consists of three parts: (1) a preliminary exploration of your personal condition before you begin, (2) the Action itself, and (3) suggestions for how it may be applied to everyday life.

Each Action leads to the next according to a definite plan, but all the Actions, without exception, are extensions and developments of the Basic Movement, which was given in Chapter IV. That movement contains the key to the whole Technique, which as we have seen is: *as you begin any movement or act, allow your whole head to move forward and upward, away from your whole body, and let your whole body delicately lengthen by following that upward direction.* It is advisable, therefore, to refer to it before undertaking a new movement.

Often the above direction is italicized within a given action. Keep in mind these and other italicized instructions throughout the Action as they are essential to the success of your experimenting.

## No Dumb-Bells, No Leotards

The Actions in this program are simple. They do not employ anything in the way of athletic equipment or apparatus. You can do them anywhere: at home or at work, in your kitchen or office. (When the weather permits, doing them outdoors will provide the additional benefit of fresh air.)

The Actions require no gym shorts, or leotards or other special outfits. Street clothes, office clothes—any clothes you happen to be wearing—are fine, and no change of apparel will be necessary afterward. Whatever clothes you do wear should, however, allow you sufficient leeway so that you are not restricted in your movements and do not feel hampered in your breathing. If your clothes are not really comfortable, you may want to loosen your shirt collar or open your belt a notch. Simply do whatever is needed to allow you to be freer in moving about and less confined in your breathing.

## A Way to Begin

Read the instructions for each Action slowly until you have an idea of what it is. (If you prefer, have someone read the instructions aloud to you.) Then proceed to carry them out in the manner described.

Sometimes the instructions are given in metaphorical language to convey what is wanted. Thus, when you are instructed to "direct your energy upward," don't worry about a scientific meaning: simply follow the instruction!

You needn't do a great many Actions at one session; you may prefer to do them gradually. For example, you may do an Action for a day or so, noticing throughout the rest of the week how that particular movement appears when it shows up in your everyday activities.

Then go on to the next Action. Initially, follow them in the order given, as each movement leads to the next according to a definite plan. Some people may prefer to do several a week. Be your own judge of your particular rate.

Later, you can always return to a given Action and see if you can discover something more in it. However often you repeat them, you will always derive some benefit, provided the element of awareness is there. Never do them mechanically; you are *not* a machine. Indeed, treating yourself like a machine is the bane of what is ordinarily meant by "exercise." Paying attention to what is happening every moment of this program reeducates your senses and muscles.

## For Your Enjoyment

Although a conscientious attitude is necessary, it is *not* necessary to drive yourself to the limits of your endurance. Indeed, that is an entirely wrong approach. It is far more beneficial to do an Action sensitively three or four times, without strain or tension, than to do it automatically many times. Remember, you are not in competition with anyone. You are doing the Action only for yourself, for your own good.

If you rush through a meal, you do not give yourself the opportunity to taste what you are eating or to digest the food properly. Ill-digested movement, like ill-digested food, is less beneficial to you. You will enjoy the Actions more if they are done in a spirit of experiment and play. You should even allow yourself a little time in which to feel and enjoy the aftereffects of each Action. Do not rush from one directly into the next.

Tall, short, thin, fat, lanky or padded, whatever the proportions of your body and whatever your age, there is nothing to prevent you from learning these Actions and doing them with enjoyment. You will adjust them to your own body as you go along.

## Nine Rules to Follow

1. Your "head" means the whole three-dimensional globe— not just your face or chin or some other part of it. (See Fig. 9, p. 39.)
2. Your "body" means the whole torso. (See Fig. 11, p. 40.)
3. "Upward" indicates a direction, not a fixed place. (See Figs. 12, 13, pp. 42 and 43.)
4. Refer to the Basic Movement (pp. 35–36) each time you proceed to a new Action.
5. Perform each Action at your own pace, not in the fastest way possible. *How* is what matters.
6. Stay alive: Keep breathing and seeing the world around you. There is no reason to hold your breath or go glassy-eyed.
7. Do not worry about executing the Actions "correctly." It is not a question of doing them the "right way,"

but rather of discovering greater flexibility and freedom in your movements.

8. Breathe easily and naturally through your nose.
9. Perform each Action as though for the first time.

# ACTION 1
# *Leaning Forward and Backward*

## Exploring Yourself

Sit in a chair and turn your head from side to side and then up and down to look around the room.

Note any sensations of which you are aware, such as a popping or crackling noise in your spine, sore muscles or stiffness. Do you really need to use your body as well as your neck to turn your head?

Lean forward and then sit back in the chair. Repeat three or four times. What parts of you tense in order to move forward and then back? Do you push yourself forward instead of letting your hip joints simply hinge? Do you hold your breath?

## Applying the Basic Movement

Still sitting, don't change your position, but look around the room by turning your head. *Let your whole head move delicately forward and up, away from your body, and pivot on the top of your spine* (top of your neck). *Let your body lengthen upward.* Notice whether or not you are able to move your head more easily and let your head move up. Involve your neck muscles as needed, but don't force your head around. Your neck will twist a little to let your head turn farther to the right or left. Then bring your head to rest.

Now that you've begun to think about how you are using your head, *include your body in that upward movement* and lean forward. (Fig. 1.) While allowing your head to continue upward and away from the top of your spine, let your body follow upward as it leans forward in space. Keep your seat; simply bend at the hips to lean forward. In leaning forward, find out the difference between pushing your head up with your body and following the upward motion of your head. Try both.

**1. Lean forward by lengthening upward.**   **2. Unnecessary pushing with your body.**

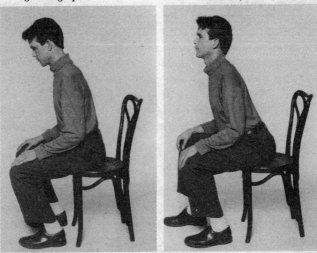

(Fig. 2.) Pay particular attention to letting your back widen toward the chair-back throughout the movement of leaning forward and you will eliminate any tendency to push.

## Applications to Daily Life

Some examples of leaning forward and back: tying your shoe while seated, reaching to turn the T.V. on or off from your chair, handing over a book or papers from a seated position and eating at the table.

### EATING SOUP

Especially watch what happens when you eat soup. The tendency is to collapse the chest and push the chin toward the bowl in order to avoid spilling the soup. (Fig. 3.) You may have tried the opposite strategy:

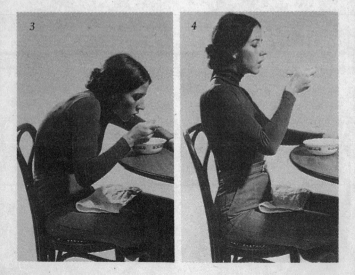

sitting very straight and trying to balance the spoon all the way to your mouth in an effort to appear graceful. (Fig. 4.) Probably the easiest way to eat soup is to lean forward effortlessly (by following your head up) and then let your torso curl slightly to bring your mouth closer to the bowl. (Fig. 5.) You will also appear more graceful and eliminate the balancing act.

## HOW TO GET OUT OF A SLUMP

"Sometimes you just want to have a good old slump," one of my teachers would often say. The next time you discover yourself in a slump, pull down a little more than you normally would. (Fig. 6.) Then experience getting out of that position by first becoming aware of a real connection between your whole head and whole body. Then begin to let your head move delicately forward and up, your body lengthening while you lean

3. *Pulling down.*

4. *Stiff, straight and awkward.*

5. *Easing upward.*

**6. The slump.**  **7. Easing upward.**

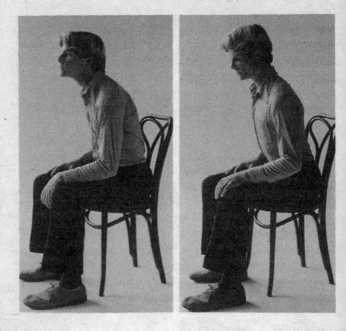

forward and then return to upright. See that you continue to allow your back to release and widen throughout the movements. (Fig. 7.) Note the change that has taken place as you emerge from your slump. You've achieved a little more ease just by moving. You can do this anytime you find yourself slouching without having to push yourself straight.

## WHEN YOU DRIVE

It is often necessary to lean forward toward the steering wheel in order to have full visibility when driving. The action of leaning forward often includes a twist as you check objects behind you. Be sure and let your head move delicately forward and your body lengthen as it twists and you'll find yourself twisting further, and with ease. Of course, driving in the normal position will also be much more pleasant if you ease up in the driver's seat.

# ACTION 2
## *Moving Arms*

### Exploring Yourself

Do this one while sitting; later, you can try it standing. Starting with your arms at your sides, lift both over your head. Then bring them down again. At first, do the movement easily enough to notice what you do with your body and head. Then try moving them quickly and in several different ways, continuing to pay attention to your head and body.

Do you tense your neck or jut your chin forward? Do you lean forward or backward with your upper torso? What parts of your body besides your arms are involved in this movement? Perhaps there are other things that you'll notice.

Every part of your body is related to every other part in movement. In other words, what you do with the remainder of your body, legs included, while you lift your arms will affect the ease and efficiency with which you can move them.

## Applying the Basic Movement

Place your hands on the tops of your thighs, palms resting down. Leave your hands there and let your arms rest comfortably at your sides. Let your head begin easing away from your body. *While your neck lengthens and your body follows the upward motion of your head,* let your arms lengthen out through your fingertips. (Figs. 1, 2, 3.) Move your hands along your legs toward your knees and let your arms float effortlessly up in front of you.

As your arms straighten out be sure and leave your elbows free and loose, not locked. Let your arms float all the way up over your head. Then let your arms come back down in front of you, hands resting on thighs, letting your elbows bend comfortably. During this entire sequence let your head rest gently on top of your spine and let your arms lengthen. No muscular stretching or reaching is required. Beware of tightening your neck, shoulders or back. (Figs. 4, 5, 6.) Think of your torso expanding upward and outward, supporting your shoulders. Repeat the movement of raising your arms, and include your torso expanding upward and outward to support your shoulders. (Fig. 7)

## Applications to Daily Life

What usually happens is that people shorten most of the muscles of any limb or any part of the body to move that part or to bend a joint. For example, to bend the elbow the way most of us do, we make a tiny jerk of the arm pulling the upper arm toward the shoulder. That

*1, 2, 3.*
*While your body follows your*
*head up, let your arms lengthen.*

**4, 5, 6.**
*No need to pull down and tighten.*

**7.** *Your shoulders move upward*
   *and outward.*

locks the elbow joint. Then we unconsciously select the
proper muscle to do the bending and use that muscle
to work against the rest of the muscles, which are
shortening. That takes a lot of extra work, and most
people do it unwittingly.

By watching how you use your arms, you will be able
to avoid a lot of excess tension that would otherwise
occur in your shoulders and neck. In the course of
your daily activities, notice how you reach to pick up
and use an object.

## BRUSHING YOUR TEETH

A good example of how most people do more work
than they need to is brushing teeth. Ask yourself if the

*8. Pulling down.*

*9. The body following the head upward.*

energy you use is really appropriate to how light a toothbrush is and the amount of pressure you need to apply to your teeth.

Next time you brush, give it some thought. See if you can make it easier. Also notice what you do with your other arm and your shoulders. (Figs. 8, 9). There is a tendency in standing activities like this one to lock your knees, which simply adds an unnecessary restriction to your freedom of movement.

## OPENING A DOOR

You can make similar observations when you open a door. Do a little experimenting to see how much strength is actually required to reach out to the knob and take hold of it. Then let your head ease up and your body follow and see if you can allow your arm to float up to the knob by lengthening out through your fingertips. (Fig. 10.) Also note if you are overdoing the action by reaching out toward the door long before you get there. (Fig. 11.)

## WITH CHILDREN

The way you use your arms in handling a young child will definitely affect how that child moves. If you are tense and nervous, a child can feel it in the way you touch him. The amount of ease you have in your own body affects almost anyone you touch, especially children.

Next time you pick up your son or daughter, think a little and notice what you are doing with yourself. Let your head move up and your arms lengthen and hold the child with the least amount of effort needed. The amount of ease from you that reaches the child will influence him to calmer and less resistant behavior.

Also important is exactly what part of the child you hold when you lift him or help him to walk or to sit. When a six-month-old child is brought up by pulling on his arms, an undue amount of tension is produced in his back and shoulders, which is maintained while the baby sits. On the other hand, if the child brings himself to sitting, he uses his whole body in a system of balances with no tension in his back or anywhere else. When you support a child with your hands in helping him to sit or stand, support him at the torso. Do not inject any effort into the easy movement the child already possesses.

# ACTION 3
## *Walking with Ease*

## Exploring Yourself

Find a room that has some open space, enough to walk around in comfortably.

From a standing position, begin to walk. Notice in which direction your energy moves. Which part of your body leads as you walk? Stop. As you start walking again, note what part of your body begins the motion and which direction you move in first: side to side? backward? forward?

Continue walking for a few minutes, stopping and starting several times until you feel that you have made some discoveries about your usual walk.

## Applying the Basic Movement

Begin standing.

As you let your head move forward and upward and away from your body with your torso following, shift

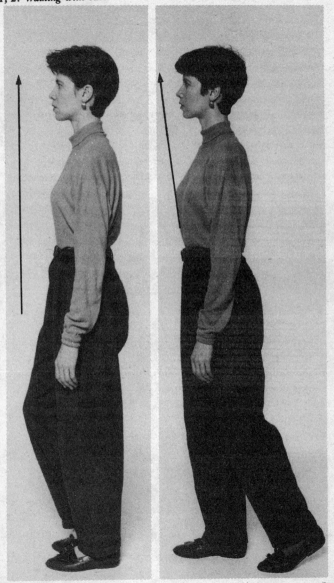

*1, 2. Walking with ease.*

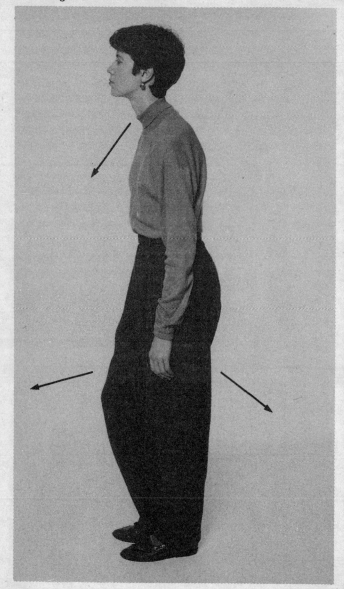

*4. Awkward, with hips forward, head dropped.*

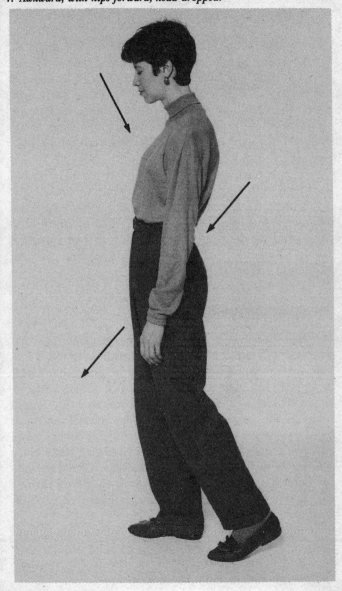

your weight onto your left foot, bend your right knee, step out with your right foot and walk forward. (Figs. 1, 2.) *When walking, the upward movement of your head and torso will move you forward;* you do not need to lean or fall forward. This will allow you to move as a unit rather than in disconnected sections—for example, hips forward, then head, then shoulders following, with each step forward consisting of an awkward fall on that foot. (Figs. 3, 4.)

Stop and start again several times. It will help if you start with both feet under you and your weight evenly distributed. *Each time you start, notice whether your head continues to ease up as you walk.* Avoid thinking of moving your head upward and then walking as two separate actions. Remember that walking and easing upward happen at the same time.

## Applications to Daily Life

My first experience with walking by means of the Alexander Technique was new and strange to me. I felt that my feet would no longer reach the floor, that I had to stretch my legs to get them down there. Once I began walking by the Alexander Technique, I discovered I was no longer pushing into my hips toward the floor on every step. Instead, I was letting my body glide along at a constant distance from the floor while continuing to explore the act of walking. I discovered my old habit had involved sinking into my hips and throwing myself off balance every time I shifted my weight from one leg to the other.

To test this for yourself, walk around the room, putting your hands at the spot on each hip where your leg bends. Place your fingers on the front side and thumbs on your middle buttocks.

Notice whether your hips shift from side to side or up and down. (There is naturally a slight, infinitesimal undulation of the hips forward and back when you walk—unless you tense up and interfere with it.)

## JOGGING AND RUNNING

With any degree of speed, there's often a tendency to pull the head back and down. (Fig. 5.) In running, therefore, whether you start at a gallop or more gradually accelerate from a walk to a run, see that you ease your head upward and allow your body to follow up after it. You'll be pleased at the gain in lightness and ease. (Fig. 6.)

## PLAYING GOLF

In golf, the upright stance provides flexibility in the shoulders and the torso and makes possible the maxi-

*5. Downward pressure.*          *6. Easing upward.*

mum control over the swing. (Fig. 7.) This important advantage is often sacrificed in the supposed interest of power. The golfer thus compacts his body, pressing in and down to brace himself in order to swing. (Fig. 8). Otherwise he fears he cannot swing hard enough.

However, it is the speed of the club head and not the force with which it is swung that makes the ball travel farthest. With a compacted approach, the golfer is getting in his own way. Only when he is willing to let his head move up and his body follow, shoulders easing out, will he maintain an upright stance and his arms have the greatest flexibility possible. His whole body will become involved in the swing, which helps increase the speed and control of it. He will then have a true one-piece swing.

# ACTION 4
## *Moving Legs*

## Exploring Yourself

Stand next to a firm waist-level surface. Rest one hand on it lightly; you may use it to balance yourself during this exploration.

Lift your right leg till your thigh is parallel to the floor. Take note of how successful you are at balancing on one leg. Now lower your leg down to the floor.

Lift and lower your right leg several times. Does your right lower leg hang as freely from your knee as it can or is it tense? Do you lift or move your right hip unnecessarily? When you lower your leg, do you release it and drop it easily or do you reach for the floor with your foot and tense the muscles in your leg as you lower it?

Once again take note of what your head and body have been doing.

## 1. Lift your leg.

## Applying the Basic Movement

Move your head and look around the room as you let your head ease forward and upward from the top of your spine and let your body follow that upward mo-

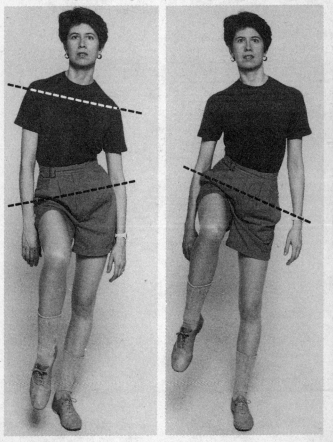

*2. Avoid sinking into the hip.*     *3. Lifting the hip needlessly.*

tion. Stop moving your head and as your body continues easing upward, bend your right knee and lift your right leg until your thigh is about parallel with the floor. (Fig. 1.) Continue to stabilize yourself when you need to by resting your hand on the firm surface nearby. Avoid sinking into the leg on which you are standing (Fig. 2) or lifting the hip of the leg being lifted. (Fig. 3.) Imagine a line drawn from one hip to the other and keep that line parallel with the floor. (Fig. 4.)

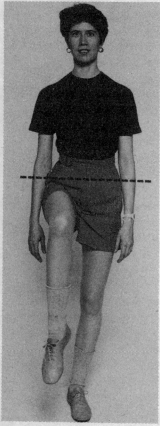

*4. The line of the hips is parallel to the floor.*

Now let your raised leg swing forward and back freely from your knee down. Push your lower leg with either hand instead of using your muscles to swing it. It should be free enough so that if someone were to push it lightly, it would swing like a pendulum until it lost momentum.

Then gently release that leg to the floor. *Before you shift any of your weight onto it, first make sure the whole sole of your foot is touching the floor,* then move your head and body upward as your weight shifts to that leg. Lift your other leg by bending the knee while letting your head and body continue upward. Let your lower leg swing freely, then gently release at the hip joint until your foot touches the floor again.

The next time you repeat lifting one of your legs, allow your foot to come to the floor in front and to the side of the foot that supports you. Then shift your weight from the back foot to the front by allowing your head to delicately move away from the top of your spine and letting your body follow that upward motion over your foot. Be careful not to narrow your back. On each step, lift your leg a shorter distance so that finally you will be walking easily. The important thing is to discover how to allow your body to go upward and forward over your legs instead of being carried by them like dead weight.

## Applications to Daily Life

### WALKING UP AND DOWN STAIRS

Many students of the Alexander Technique find that walking up or down stairs makes them realize how much less effort is needed when directing their energy upward.

People have pre-set attitudes toward almost every

physical task they perform. These attitudes generally involve erroneous judgment of how much effort is required to perform a task or how their bodies must work to do it well. The error occurs when a person doesn't experiment with his attitude—doesn't try out easier ways to do the job. Examine your attitude toward climbing stairs. How much effort is necessary to get up to the next step? A typical attitude held is that a person must push downward in order to move *up* to the next step. So the direction of energy is often downward when a person climbs stairs. (Fig. 5.) The problem occurs during the shift of weight after the foot has been lifted to the next stair. Most people place all their weight onto the forward foot before straightening the leg, and the effort involved in straightening the leg with most of the body weight on it is exhausting. To climb stairs the Alexander Technique way, place your foot

5. *Downward direction.*          6. *Upward direction.*

lightly on the step and gradually straighten your leg as you follow your head upward and forward to move your body above that stair. (Fig. 6.)

Walking down stairs is often done with equal inefficiency, usually because it is never approached consciously. To move down a staircase, simply allow your knee to bend forward as you follow your head upward. (Fig. 7, 8.) There is no need to keep the muscles of your knee in constant tension to serve as a brake; nor do you need to jump from foot to foot, which requires extra work in order to maintain balance and control.

When you are walking up or down stairs, allowing your head to move forward and upward and your body to follow, you can still look down at the stairs to see where you are stepping. Avoid freezing your gaze. In going up an incline, apply the same principles.

*7. Pulling down.*            *8. Easing upward.*

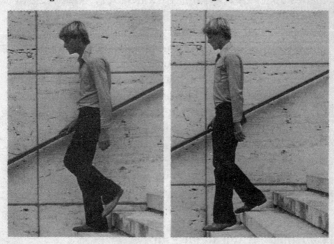

# ACTION 5
## *Heel and Toe*

## Exploring Yourself

Sit in a chair, rest your feet on the floor about five inches apart and pointing forward. Very slowly, one at a time, lift each heel off the floor and put it down again. Leave the ball and toes of your foot on the floor.

Notice whether or not the movement is smooth. You may notice that as you move your ankle, it moves as though it were on a ratchet, such as a car jack, in little jerks, up and down. This indicates excess tension and that you are tensing the muscles around your ankle.

See if you are locking your ankle joint at the top of the movement—with heel as high as possible—and at the end of the movement—with foot flat on the floor.

When your heel comes up, where does the pressure on the ball of your foot fall? Is it under your big toe, in the center, on the outside or evenly across the front of your foot, as is most desirable? Do you have to tense your thigh or calf to lift your heel?

Also try slowly lifting your toes off of the ground so that only your heel remains on the floor. Look for the same indications of freedom or tension.

## Applying the Basic Movement

Begin as before with your feet at least five inches apart and pointing forward in whatever position is most comfortable. (Fig. 1.) Sit comfortably and turn your head from side to side. Now *as you let your head move delicately forward and upward and away from your body and allow your body to follow,* include your legs in your awareness. Think of your whole leg getting longer, between your hip socket and your knee and between your ankle and your knee. Then stop turning your head. Avoid contracting the muscles of your thigh by *continuing to allow your leg to lengthen* as your left heel comes very slowly off the floor as far as it can. Keep the ball of your foot on the ground and spread your toes. (Fig. 2.) Then as you let your heel very gently down to the floor, release your ankle and continue lengthening your bent leg. This does not mean stretching your leg, but rather to allow it to be its full length and free of tension. See if you can find the most efficient way (the one involving the least tension) to raise and lower your heel.

Now see what happens when you repeat this action. There is no set way to do it. It will either become easier, be unchanged or become tiring. But something constructive is happening; you are becoming aware of how you move your ankle. When you understand how easing your head upward and letting your body follow affects the movement of your ankle and every other part of your body, you will begin to improve your use of yourself.

If you concentrate solely on your ankles to the exclusion of the rest of your body, it will be harder to move them freely. Remain aware of the relationship between your head and body, and let the movement of your ankles fit in with it. The body's motions can now be consistent from the top of your head to the tip of your toes.

Now lift your toes off the ground so that only your heel remains on the floor. Let your toes bend slightly up from the floor, then let the remainder of your foot, except your heel, follow upward. (Fig. 3.) In order to begin and complete this movement, let your head ease upward and follow it with your body. Lengthen your leg all the way from heel to hip. As you continue, let your toes come back to the floor. Repeat with your

*1. Foot flat on floor pointing forward.*

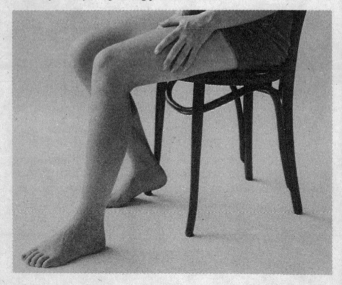

## 2. *Lift your heel.*

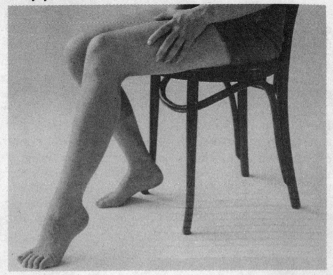

## 3. *Lift your toes.*

other foot. Then stand up and walk around to see what changes have occurred.

## Applications to Daily Life

Freedom in your ankles is essential for efficient and easy walking, but there is no need to focus on them except when doing this Action. Generally, the upward direction of your head and body, now including your legs and feet, will give you added freedom of motion.

# ACTION 6
## *Knee-Bending*

### Exploring Yourself

Stand with your feet shoulders' width apart (from twelve to eighteen inches). Have your feet nearly parallel but not quite. They should be pointing just an inch outward from parallel at the toes.

Bend both knees until they are directly above your big toe, keeping your body perpendicular to the ground. Then straighten your legs and return to the standing position.

Notice where you feel any pressure on your hips or legs. Notice what if anything you do with your head and your body. Are you bending at the hips and ankles? Repeat this until you are clear about how you are bending your knees.

## Applying the Basic Movement

*Allow your head to move delicately upward, away from your body, and allow your body to follow.* Include your legs in the easing so that they lengthen and lighten. As you release the muscles around your knees, let them go forward. (Fig. 1.) A common tendency is to think of the knees as moving downward, which creates more pressure than is necessary. Instead, make sure they fold directly forward above each foot. When you are successful with this Action, you will feel no pressure or strain on your knees.

As your knees bend, continue to follow your head upward with your body and without tightening your legs. Your legs shuld continue to lengthen as your knees bend. Make sure you release your hip joints so that your body does not tilt backward when your hips lock (Fig. 2), or forward if needless extra effort is used in bending your hips (Fig. 3), but remains perpendicular to the ground (Fig. 1).

Rather than pushing your body back up with your legs, let your head and body ease upward from your legs and let your knees follow.

Keep your body sense alert so that you can tell if at any point you are tensing your knees. Don't let your old habits interfere with your new way of bending.

## Applications to Daily Life

The simultaneous bending of both knees rarely occurs by itself in everyday activity; rather, it is part of the movement of sitting and standing. If you're a dancer,

*1. Release knees forward.*

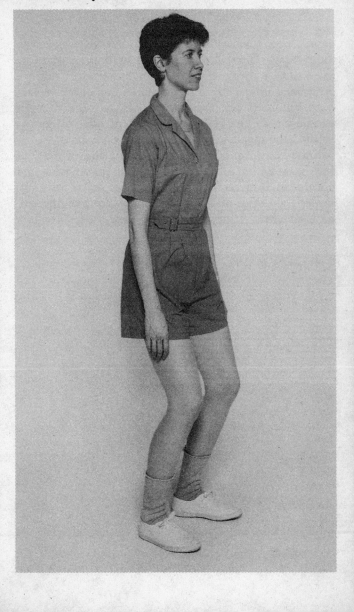

you will encounter a variation of it in the plié. When people bend to pick up things, and do the work with their legs as they should instead of their backs, that movement is present even though their feet may be positioned differently. The greatest value of this Action is that it frees the hips and knees, a freedom most people need. The act of walking is greatly influenced by the amount of flexibility in the leg joints.

Knee-bending is also the most efficient way of approaching any activity in which you are standing and must lean over to work. Working at a low counter, carpentry, doing dishes and ironing are examples of such activities. Instead of going forward by bending

*2. No need to tilt back.*

*3. No need to lean forward.*

your back and hunching your shoulders (Fig. 4.), stay upright and bend your knees to lower yourself to the level you need. (Fig. 5.)

*4. Pulling down.*

*5. Easing upward, knees bent.*

# ACTION 7
# *Standing Up and Sitting Down*

## Exploring Yourself

In Action 1, you learned how to lean forward without pushing forward. Now get up from a chair, noticing what your body must do in order to stand. When leaning forward in order to stand up, do you use more effort than when you merely lean forward in a chair? No more effort is actually needed.

Now sit down from a standing position and notice what happens to the relationship of your head to your body. Do you freeze your head or any part of your body while you sit?

Repeat these two Actions, noting everything that is involved in sitting and standing.

## Applying the Basic Movement

*Standing Up.* Sit in a chair of average height. Begin by becoming aware of what you do with your head and

*1. Following your head upward.*

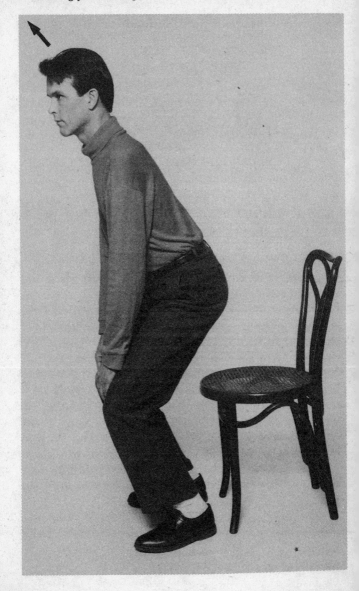

your body. Turn your head from side to side and allow
it to move forward and up and away from your body.
*As you become aware of the forward and upward direction,
lean forward by following your head with your body.* Continue
following as you lean forward until your buttocks come
off the chair. (Fig. 1.) As you lean forward, "upward"
becomes diagonal from the chair, not skyward. As soon
as your legs are straightened out, you have completed
the movement.

Sit back in the chair and repeat this movement several times, noticing what you do in order to come to your
feet. Discover how to do the movement in one flowing
motion with the least possible effort. Often people
discover that they are giving a little push, a little
tightening, just before they leave the chair. There are
many people who at first feel that this little push is
absolutely necessary but soon discover it isn't when they
let their bodies follow their heads.

Having made a slight improvement in the flow from
sitting to getting your buttocks off the chair, go all the
way to standing the next time you do it. "Upward" will
continually change in relation to vertical as you fold
forward. Notice whether you continue to follow your
head or whether you change direction and push yourself up. (Fig. 2.) Beware of trying to swing yourself to
your feet. (Fig. 3.)

NOTE: When you stand, it is necessary to use your
thigh muscles to some extent, so rather than concentrate on your legs, observe what you must do with your
head and body to gain the most efficient use of your
legs.

*After you have come to a standing position, your head
continues upward and your body continues to follow it.* There
is no reason to abandon that upward direction and
collapse after you have stood up. (Fig. 4.)

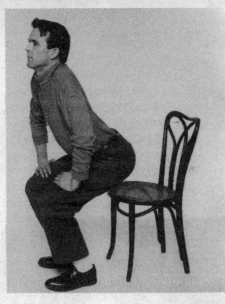

2. *Beware of pushing.*

3. *Beware of swinging up.*

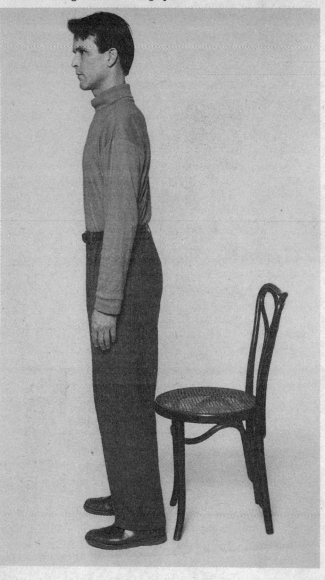

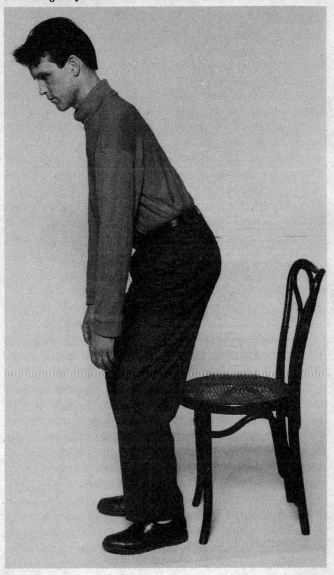

5. *Bending the joints to sit.*

*Sitting Down.* In the act of sitting, the advantage of following your head with your body is that you have control of your balance as you sit. An important idea to grasp about sitting *down* is that you must *continue to follow your head upward with your body.* If you let all your joints fold as you sit, and direct the energy upward to relieve pressure on the joints instead of tensing to keep from falling, you will not have to work as hard.

As you stand in front of a chair, get your head and body going upward. As soon as you feel pressure taken off your legs, release your leg joints and let them fold. Remember to let your hips bend as well so that you lean forward as you approach the chair. (Fig. 5.) If this is confusing, stand up again, noting how far you fold forward as you stand. Sitting down is the same movement in reverse.

## Applications to Daily Life

Of the movements we repeat most often, one that uses the whole body is the movement from standing to sitting and vice versa. Most of us complete this action many times a day in an uncountable number of ways and positions. Whichever way it is done, though, it is all the same basic movement: bending at the hips, knees and ankles, then folding into the chair to sit; unfolding the joints and rebalancing the weight on the feet to stand. It is one of the best movements you can do to explore coordination of your whole body.

Most people drop themselves into a chair and push themselves out. How many people have you seen who push their knees down with their hands in trying to stand, when they actually need their legs to go up? (Fig. 2.) Without even thinking about it, many people divide the movement of standing into steps: lean forward, push down, shoot up. They go through a sequence that resembles shifting gears in a 1950 pickup. But if you can learn to follow your head with your body, you can avoid the shifts in direction and stand up in one easy flowing motion. You will still have the flexibility to twist and turn your head, reach out with your arms or perform any other variation on the movement of standing. And you can do it without the extra effort of forcing or tensing your muscles.

## Some Words About Talking

How you talk is affected by the amount of compression and tension in your neck, head, and body. When you learn to follow the upward direction of your head with your whole body you will also be freeing your breathing. (See pp. 26-28.) Greater freedom in breathing brings greater freedom in speaking.

Read aloud from a book or recite a simple nursery rhyme while sitting comfortably in a chair. How do you use your head, neck, and torso? Do you leave them free or do you pull them down? Do you stiffen your neck or does your head rest loosely on top of your neck? Do you gasp air in through your mouth or do you let it flow in through your nose?

Discover what happens when you think of your whole head moving delicately upward and your whole body lengthening. Let a new breath flow in through your nose, then, as you continue to direct your head to move upward, speak again. If you continue easing up while you speak you will discover how much easier speaking can be.

## The Whispered "Ah"

Whenever you read aloud or speak you can allow the sound to flow out of you just as easily as breath flows out. Practice letting your breath flow out along the roof of your mouth. Whispering an "ah" sound can give you a chance to coordinate free and easy movement in your jaw, your neck and spine and your breath. The command of a rich, full voice will be yours both in ordinary social conversation and on those occasions when you may have to address a larger group.

First check the flexibility of your jaw by very gently placing your fingertips on your chin just below your

6. & 7.

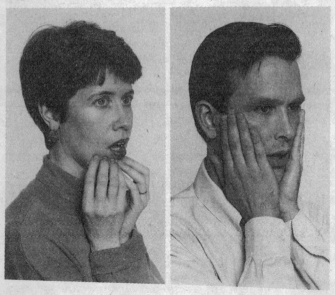

lower lip, with your thumbs on the underside of your jaw. (Fig 6.) Leaving the jaw muscles loose and resting, now slowly open and close your mouth with your fingertips. Then quickly and lightly shake your jaw up and down in the same manner. If your jaw resists during this easy test, it is likely that you hold tension in your jaw and tongue muscles when you speak.

You can change this situation with a simple procedure. Make sure that as you perform it your whole head delicately moves forward and upward while your whole body lengthens. Cradle your jaw in your hands by placing your thumbs under the back corners of your jaw and placing your fingertips in front of your ears. The heels of your hands will be together at your chin. Slowly open your mouth using your hands on your lower jaw. (Fig. 7.) Then close your mouth again using your hands to do so and when your lips are brought together breathe in. Lower your jaw once more and let your breath flow out through your open mouth as your body continues to delicately follow the upward direction of your head. Think of your breath as flowing out along the roof of your mouth. It will sound just like you are whispering the syllable "ah."

Once you've found out what it's like to open your mouth without any muscular effort (by using your hands) you can simply allow your jaw to release open without your hands. Try it. Then whisper "ah" without using your hands. After you've done two or three whispered "ahs" let the fourth whisper turn into a sounded "ah". See that you continue allowing your head to move forward and upward and your body to follow. Each time you need to breathe, close your lips and let air flow in. When reading aloud, talking on the phone, singing or speaking you can let your voice flow out just like the sounded "ah." Eventually any time you use your voice you'll be using the Alexander Technique with ease.

## Encouraging Children

John Dewey, the esteemed educator and thinker, said that Alexander's discovery and method of procedure is perfect for the young. So if you are a parent or work with children you can share this easy way of using ourselves with all ages. From infancy to the age of five no formal teaching need be done. Simply handle the children with thoughtfulness (see pages 84–85) and set a good example for them to mimic by using the Technique yourself.

By the age of five or six children are ready and delighted to explore the use of themselves. Five to ten minutes at a time is all it takes to encourage their awareness of tension versus ease.

First you can find out what they already notice about what people do with their bodies when they are tense. (I have been amazed at how accurate kindergarteners are in describing the lifted shoulders, scrunched neck of someone who is tense.) Suggest to them that by letting their heads delicately float up and their bodies lengthen they can actually lessen the amount of tension they have. Instead of using the word lengthen you may want to talk about how their body gets longer or taller and expands outward. Children tend to be remarkably apt in accepting the idea that the head leads and the body follows.

Using the gentle movements in "A Short Daily Routine" with children during rest period, or quiet time after gym, can also encourage children's physical awareness and their ability to release tension. Often just thinking about letting the neck be easy, the head float away from the top of the spine, and letting the body lengthen will do the trick and children will feel lighter and calmer on returning to their activities.

# A
# Short
# Daily Routine

## A Time for Rest

The experiments you've been doing thus far have been designed to teach you conscious control of yourself. The point of it all is to teach you to let your head and body ease *upward* during *any* movement.

There is one activity you can use daily to reinforce the process of lengthening in movement. Begin by finding a place that is comfortable, relatively quiet and can be used regularly. Plan to use this space whenever you want to do this activity. Lie down with your feet flat on the floor and your knees bent. Ideally, your feet should be a shoulders' width apart and your knees balanced freely, directly above your feet. (Fig. 1.) More realistically, your knees will tend to fall toward each other, or outward, spread-eagle fashion. See if you can get your knees to fall inward rather than outward. Putting your feet farther apart is helpful.

Let your feet rest parallel to each other on the floor

and about two feet away from your buttocks. If any of these positions creates undue pressure, then make minor adjustments. Make yourself comfortable on your back, feet on the floor. As you learn to direct energy upward and to move with greater freedom, it will become easier to lie down this way. Keep your eyes open.

Let your arms rest easily on the floor at your sides, or bend them at the elbows and rest your hands comfortably on your stomach. A two-inch thick pillow under your head is permissible, though you'll soon be able to rest without one. Simply lie there for two to five minutes. (When you are feeling extremely tense, you may need up to twenty minutes.) As you lie there, make a mental note of your body's condition. Afterward, write down the things you noticed during each session, so you can compare your awareness from one week to the next. For example:

> Pressure across the back of my hips
> Tingling in my right knee
> Pain in my left upper back
> Sensation along the left side of my neck

*1. Lie down.*

The floor is cold on my back
My breathing moves my stomach
The small of my back isn't touching the floor
Feeling a little angry at first
Cold fingers
Felt calmer at the end, warmer

More than likely you'll notice the same things from day to day, but continue to make note of them each time. You may also be able to remember all these sensations. In that case you do not need to write your notes but can use your memory instead.

What is important here is that you have begun to spend a period every day, short though it may be, on body maintenance. When you have made a change in your belief system, from "I have too many important things to do, and too many responsibilities, for me to be spending time on myself," to "time spent on myself is as important as any other time," you can give yourself the opportunity to improve your performance of any activity.

After you've taken this thoughtful rest for a few minutes, let your head move away from your body and let your body lengthen from buttocks to shoulders. Let your shoulders widen and open. You don't need to push your body into changing. You may, however, find that your body does begin to lengthen, but because of friction with the floor you feel stuck at first. If that should happen, do the following series of movements to allow your body to continue lengthening.

1. With the back of your head touching the floor at all times, move your head by nodding it, chin toward your chest and then back up from your chest, several times. All the while you are doing this, your head continues to move *delicately* away from your body. After nodding, let your head come to rest in a position where

your neck, front and back, seems to have some length.

2. Lift your right shoulder toward the ceiling. As you release it back to the floor, move it slightly out from your body. Again, the shoulder, front and back, will feel slightly longer. Do the same with your left shoulder.

3. With your feet firmly on the floor, lift your hips up from the floor. The lift continues to the middle of the back. Then starting at the middle back, slowly lower your body until your hips are on the floor again. (Fig. 2.)

Now that you do not feel stuck to the floor, you're ready to experiment with some movements in the lying-down position. During all of the following movements think of your head moving delicately away from the top of your spine and your body lengthening. Leave your neck free at all times.

## Rotating Your Head

See how easily you can rotate your head from side to side. Observe whether any other part of your body tightens or moves as you roll your head. Move your head by letting it ease away from your body and, as that begins to lengthen your neck, roll your head from side to side. Be careful not to increase the pressure of your head against the floor. Find a way to move without jerking or setting (tensing) your body. Use the release of tension to move your head. Roll it from side to side a few times.

Continue to experiment with moving your head, rolling it from side to side. Try doing fast movements with the least amount of tensing. Any movement can be done by letting your head ease upward and your body follow. There is no need to tense any part of your body to start the movement.

## Moving Your Arms

Lift your arms one at a time, beginning the movement by easing your head upward. Very gently lengthen out through your fingertips. Permit your shoulders to continue easing outward from your body. First let your hand float from the floor, bending your wrist (Fig. 3.) Then allow your lower arm to float up, following your hand and bending your elbow. (Fig. 4.) Finally your upper arm can follow the floating movement and your whole arm will be above your body. (Fig. 5.) Straighten your arm. Bend it and curve it any way you wish. All of the movements can be effortless.

Let your other arm rise the same way. Make sure you move your arm without a jolt or locking any part of it. Pay attention to what you do with your head and body as you move your arm. Notice whether or not you press your head into the floor or lift it off the floor slightly to move your arm.

Then slowly and gently move *both* arms in every which way. See what happens when you move your

## 3. First move your hand.

## 4. Then the lower arm moves.

## 5. Move your whole arm.

arms quickly and sharply. Don't interfere with the freedom you've created in your head, body and arms.

Whenever you let your arms return to the floor, first
allow your upper arm to come to the floor. As you let it
down gently, lengthen it toward your elbow. There's no
need to push it away from your body. Then let your
lower arm follow and, finally, your hand, continuing
the movements of ease.

## Moving Your Legs

Next lift your legs one at a time. Direct the energy up
through the bent knee toward the ceiling, allowing your
head to move away from your body as your body
follows. Lift one foot off the floor by bringing your leg
toward your chest. (Fig. 6.) Your knee will travel through
a slight arc. Then place your foot on the floor again.
Do this a couple of times with each leg, noticing where
you tighten and observing whether or not you tense
your head as you move your leg. Return always to the
bent-knee position.

Now lift your left leg again and bring your leg
toward your chest. Then as your leg moves away from
your chest again, let your left foot slide along the floor
away from your body until it is straightened and fully

*6. Bring your leg toward your chest.*

on the floor. (Fig. 7.) Let your right leg straighten in the same manner.

The object is to learn to move your legs with the least amount of tightening in your stomach, back and whole body. Leaving your feet on the ground draw your knees up again, one at a time, while thinking of your legs lengthening outward through your knees. Allow the ease to continue in your head, neck and torso.

## Rolling onto Your Side

Let your knees fall slowly and easily to one side. To do this, let your head begin rolling toward the same side. (Fig. 8.) As your head continues to move, let your knees come to the floor, causing your body to roll until you are lying on your side. (Fig. 9.) Then roll onto your back by moving your head first and letting your whole body follow. Roll to the opposite side in the same manner. Always let your head and neck be free.

## Getting Up

To sit up from the lying position, roll onto your side. Let your head move away from your body and let your

7. *The leg is straightened.*

**8. Let your head roll to the side.**

**9. Your knees roll to the floor.**

body move with it. Use the arm closer to the ceiling to push on the floor in front of your chest. (Fig. 9.) Now you should be sitting. As you sit up, it is essential to let your head continue moving instead of locking in place. Seated it's easy to stand simply by following your head with your body.

Remember, your head doesn't necessarily have to be the highest part of your body as you stand. If you want to bend over as you come up, let your head go outward from the top of your spine and permit your body to follow. Now straighten up, doing the same.

## Restful Slumber

Sometimes we do not get the full benefit of a good night's sleep because we continue so many of our habits of tension while we sleep. The best way to sleep is on your back unless you have specific physical problems that prevent this position. Having a good soft pillow that forms to your head, or no pillow at all, is better than a stiff or bouncy one.

When you first lie down, use the position of rest described above (Fig. 1.). Then let your legs straighten out and rest on the mattress as you continue to let your head move away and your body to follow it.

If you must sleep on your side, a few adjustments will make this position more advantageous. Bunch your pillow under the side of your head so that your neck is straight as it would be in standing. This will keep your body from collapsing onto the shoulder that rests on the mattress and will prevent your neck from cramping (Figs. 10, 11). Then lay your top arm on the side of your body, or at least rest the upper part of it on your upper side, and let it bend at the elbow. This way your upper shoulder does not curl down, collapsing onto your chest (Fig. 11.), but rests directly above the other shoulder with your chest and back unconstricted.

When rising from the bed in the morning, avoid doing any movement, such as a sit-up, that can shock your body with exaggerated muscle action. If you slept on your back, first roll onto your side, then sit up gently as you ease your head and body up. If you must do them in the morning, do all your exercises *after* your body is more awake and your heart has adjusted its beat to a moving body.

*10. Lengthening.*

*11. Cramped.*

## Emotional Control—Worry, Anger, Panic

You can apply the Alexander Technique in your daily life so that your emotions do not get out of hand. Emotions are not the result of a conscious decision; they arise subconsciously before the conscious mind can act. The value of control can be seen if we recall for a moment the many unfortunate events in which we and those we love have been hurt by actions stemming from fear, anger or hostility.

Any harmful, wasteful or debilitating emotion will express itself in tensions that you can perceive even before you go haywire, inundated by it. Anger, for instance, even before you choke up or explode, tenses muscles in the neck, jaw and shoulders, among others. When you detect these signals, simply give some attention to easing your head upward and allowing your body to follow after it. This is not the same as trying to *suppress* anger, which can tie you into knots or make matters worse. Rather, the new direction of your energy, by releasing tension throughout your body, gives you a means of coping with the emotion so that it remains a potential for action but does not interfere with rational decision and any action you may take.

By this procedure you can, for example, eliminate the panic from fear and size up the situation that inspires it and do something about it.

# Some
# Helpful
# Hints

You now have the simple program that will make an important change in how you function at every level of your daily life. You have learned a very new way of thinking and moving.

But perhaps because the Alexander Technique is so easy to do, we manufacture unnecessary difficulties in the process of learning it. The reason may be that it seems too good to be true: it can't be that simple. Surely there have got to be complications, and so we go about inventing them.

As a teacher of the Alexander Technique, I have encountered many of the handicaps that people create for themselves at the beginning. Following are some of the needless difficulties I have most often observed.

These thumbnail portraits have been designed as a series of helpful hints for carrying out the Technique. It may be that you are not troubled in any of the ways described below. If so, well and good. But perhaps you may discover one or another obstacle with which you have been needlessly hampering your own progress in acquiring the Technique. If that is the case, take careful note of the sketch that applies to you, the problem involved and the answer to it. The entire purpose of the sketches that follow is to provide a means for understanding and resolving any unnecessary problem you may recognize in yourself. It can be eliminated as soon as you become aware of it, and it need not impede the smooth course of making the Alexander Technique your own.

## The Worrier

One of the most common tendencies seen in beginners is the "I can't" habit. These people focus on what they won't or can't do. When, for example, they give their bodies the instruction to follow their heads, they immediately ask themselves, "Am I doing it?" They notice that nothing is happening and then they think, "I'm not doing it! I can't."

The idea of the Alexander Technique is to pay attention to what you *are* doing. Are you pulling down? Then go up. Don't worry about what you're *not* doing. In other words, it's not necessary to be in a state of continual regret when you feel you're in error. Thinking about how you should be easing up is like making a plan to do the laundry instead of actually doing it.

## The Straining Housewife

One of my own experiences can best explain what is involved here. I was in the kitchen one day, after spending an entire morning teaching the Technique and talking a lot about integrating relaxation into daily activity. While scrubbing away furiously at a burned pot and considering all this, I suddenly thought, "Why not practice what you preach?" So I let my head move up and my body follow. In the process, I realized I had been bent over, pulling my shoulders in.

As I stood there, feeling very easy, I let my arm lengthen and hold onto the scrub brush very lightly. I experimented with just how hard I needed to hold onto it, and began to press more lightly on the pot. It was still coming clean. As I stood there, feeling better and better, guilt crept over me. This can't be right if it's making me feel good instead of strained and tired, I reasoned. Still, I continued my experiment until the pot was clean and then I felt actually refreshed.

After that experience, I began to notice a definite physical attitude that took over whenever I worked in the kitchen or performed other household chores. Every activity had a different but usually effortful physical attitude attached to it. Only by thinking during the activity was I able to avoid doing the excess work that made me feel I was doing the job right. There really is no need to be a "straining housewife."

## The Thinker

She says: "I think and think about my head going up but nothing happens."

I tell her: You have not quite understood what I mean by "thinking." It is not just the process of repeating the words or idea in your head. Thinking in these terms must be an active process that actually releases you from the downward pulls you ordinarily experience. Let it happen. Go past words to experiencing the idea.

## The Scientist

He had deduced: "My head and body can only go so far upward before levitating is the next step. How can words possibly make them go farther when you reach that limit?"

What he has forgotten is that upward is a direction, not a place. There is a maximum point of lengthening the spine, but you can always continue to direct your head upward as you continue to move about. This presents the tendency to pull it downward.

## The Manipulator

"When I get a tension headache, I can force . . . well, do it with my hands. I can stretch my neck by putting one hand under my chin, the other hand on my shoulder, and pushing my head up. But I can't keep hanging on that way. When I take my hands off, my head comes back down again."

Obviously, you can't go around doing that and carry on your everyday activities. But you can do some constructive thinking that carries over into every activity. Direct your head to move upward and your body to follow with awareness, not hands.

## The Under-Achiever

The under-achiever says: "Oh, it takes so much energy to stay aware and remember to move 'Up.' I can't go around thinking about this all the time. I have things to do, and it's very hard to do two things at once."

Preventing the back-and-down pull is like breaking

any other habit. At first you have to remind yourself to do something different—in this case, to move your head up. Soon this awareness will become an integral part of everything you do. You won't have to summon the thought to move your head; it will be there.

## The Step-by-Stepper

He says: "I ease up every time before I move, but I just look as though I'm being stiff and formal."

To the step-by-stepper I reply: See if you can ease up in order to make a move rather than easing up *before* you move. That way change will come out of every activity you do and not as a result of something imposed on you. If you do this, then "up" becomes relative to the movement you're doing. If you bend over, your head can still move up away from your body but of course not toward the ceiling. The next step, then, will be to learn to continue directing the energy upward during the movement.

## The Freezer

He declares: "I know where up is, and when I'm sitting still and not doing anything, I can remember to think about it. But as soon as I move, I think about that immediate move and forget about easing up. Surely I have to do something, tense some muscles, to get forward in a chair."

When you're letting your head ease up and your body follow, you're already moving, so all you have to do is continue moving and you'll get to where you want to be. You still have to learn how to recognize your own movement without tensing or pulling down. I think of any action as moving upward with my head and body. For example, I go up with my head and let my body follow to reach with my arm in *any* direction.

## The Over-Achiever

He has the opposite problem from the under-achiever: "When I do what I think is easing up and maintain, hold it, I feel very uncomfortable and stiff. I try to think about it all the time, and then I feel as though I shouldn't move or I'll lose it. So I don't turn my head, and I don't ever slouch in a chair."

Whenever you think you're doing something right, let go of it. You yourself change from movement to movement as do the requirements of any activity in which you may be engaged. What *you* do is make your head move up as far as possible, then when you get to the limit, you tense up, lock in and become inflexible. The point of asking you to let your head ease upward and your body to follow is that you can get a little more *flexibility* and *ease*. When you get to the point where you refuse to change, you've lost that flexibility.

The fact is, you're easing up as soon as you think of it. That's fine. The change you can make yourself is very subtle. Be satisfied with a little so that you notice the smaller changes more.

## The Detailer

He insists upon thinking of himself as a collection of parts and there seem to be so many. "I just can't think of more than one thing at a time!" he says. Struggle as he may he can't seem to remember all of his body parts at once.

For most people, learning to think of ourselves as a whole rather than a collection of body parts is an essential feature of learning the Alexander Technique. It won't hurt for your awareness to bounce around like a pinball game from part to part as you begin to teach yourself. You will, however, become even more successful in moving easily when you learn to direct your whole head and your whole body together. Remember your head is attached to your body; when your head moves your body naturally follows.

## The Practicer

She complains: "I go home and practice this Technique every day. I do ten minutes in the morning and ten after dinner. I can really move forward and back in the chair very well, but I don't seem to be making any change. I still feel just as tense after a long day at the office as I always did. Maybe I'm practicing wrong."

First, stop practicing, and start living! In studying the Alexander principle, you're trying to learn to use yourself better. And when do you use yourself most? In all your everyday activities—eating, talking to a friend, taking a shower. These are the things you do over and over again, probably without awareness. When you start allowing your head to ease upward and your body to follow while you wash your hands, for example, then you'll be putting what you've learned to use.

You don't have to think during all activity. But every once in a while, notice and see if you can feel a little more ease. Then you're giving yourself a choice you never knew you had before—the choice of acting with or without tension.

## The Posture-Maker

She says: "I can't seem to remember where to put my head to get back that floating feeling. Where is it again? Sometimes I decide to pull my chin in and push my shoulders back but they never.seem to stay. And should my feet come down heel first or toe first?"

There is no right place to put your head, body, shoulders, chin or anything else. The Alexander principle is a principle of *movement,* not of posture and position. It just so happens that when you stop interfering with your body's natural functioning, you stand up straighter.

Go back to letting your head move upward and away from your body as your body follows, in any movement you do; for example, in taking a step. Then you're on the right track.

## The Weight-Watcher

Her reasonable question is: "You say that if I use the Alexander Technique I'll learn how to put less energy into doing everything. Won't I get flabby and out of shape if I stop exerting as much energy? Then I'll have to exercise twice as much."

You're making the wrong assumption if you think that simply putting forth energy will keep you in shape. It's the way you *use* the energy that can be of help to your body. Habitual tension doesn't keep you in shape;

it just makes for hard, locked muscle tissue. Because of unnecessary tension in certain parts of your body, some muscles don't get used at all, and usually they become a deposit area of flabby fat. When you learn to use your body as an integrated whole, then you'll get the maximum use out of all your muscles, whatever you do.

# About the Author

SARAH BARKER currently teaches in the Department of Theater Arts at the University of Pittsburgh in Pittsburgh, Pennsylvania. She received her master's in fine arts from Southern Methodist University and her Alexander Technique certification from Marjorie Barstow. Since 1974 Ms. Barker has worked in university music, athletics, performing arts departments and theatre companies throughout the nation as teacher, actress and director. Sarah Barker is internationally recognized as a leader in the field of Movement Training for Actors and has distinguished herself through her unique presentation of the Alexander Technique. Ms. Barker also conducts training in integrated learning techniques for primary and secondary school teachers and their students.

# BANTAM NEW AGE BOOKS

Bantam New Age Books are for all those interested in reflecting on life today and life as it may be in the future. This important new imprint features stimulating works in fields from biology and psychology to philosophy and the new physics.